"Sit

Stunned because he knew her name, Jenny never considered disobeying. "What do you want? If you're looking for a cheap pick-up, you're wasting your time."

A suggestion of a smile teased the corners of his mouth. "You do yourself an injustice; you look anything but cheap. Come with me."

Only as he stopped before a motel room door and pulled a key out of his pocket did Jenny's anger give way to fear. He took her arm and pulled her inside.

"After all, Jenny," he was saying, "you owe me for the truck. And there's more than one way to pay a bill. . . ."

BROOKE HASTINGS
is an avid reader who loves to travel. She draws her material from many sources: the newspaper, politics, the places she visits and the people she meets. Her unique plots, full of real people who meet love in many guises, make her one of the best new writers in this field.

Dear Reader:

Silhouette Romances is an exciting new publishing venture. We will be presenting the very finest writers of contemporary romantic fiction as well as outstanding new talent in this field. It is our hope that our stories, our heroes and our heroines will give you, the reader, all you want from romantic fiction.

Also, *you* play an important part in our future plans for Silhouette Romances. We welcome any suggestions or comments on our books and I invite you to write to us at the address below.

So, enjoy this book and all the wonderful romances from Silhouette. They're for *you!*

Karen Solem
Editor-in-Chief
Silhouette Books
P.O. Box 769
New York, N.Y. 10019

BROOKE HASTINGS
Desert Fire

Silhouette *Romance*

Published by Silhouette Books New York

America's Publisher of Contemporary Romance

Other Silhouette Romances by Brooke Hastings

Playing for Keeps
Innocent Fire

America's Publisher of Contemporary Romance

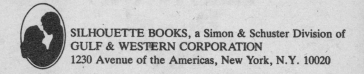

**SILHOUETTE BOOKS, a Simon & Schuster Division of
GULF & WESTERN CORPORATION**
1230 Avenue of the Americas, New York, N.Y. 10020

Copyright © 1980 by Brooke Hastings

Distributed by Pocket Books

ISBN: 0-671-57044-7

First Silhouette printing November, 1980

10 9 8 7 6 5 4 3 2 1

America's Publisher of Contemporary Romance

Printed in the U.S.A.

For Jenny and Brian

Chapter One

"These truck drivers think they own the roads!" Jennifer Ross glanced to the top of the long incline she was ascending, taking in the double row of cars, trucks, vans and recreational vehicles spaced out along her side of the four-lane highway. An enormous truck, hauling two long trailers filled with produce, had just come roaring up behind her in the left-hand lane. The driver had tailgated her impatiently until there was the merest suggestion of a break in the traffic. He had then given a thunderous blast of his horn, intimidating a half-terrified Jenny into cutting back into the right-hand lane. She had been traveling several miles faster than the legal 55 miles per hour and the truck driver must have exceeded her speed by a good ten miles.

Jennifer had a volatile, quick-tempered streak in her nature that asserted itself whenever someone attempted to dominate her. Her first instinct was to flash a rude gesture at the overbearing driver. She suppressed it. These truck drivers were a tough lot, and she had no wish to court trouble.

Jenny had been driving south for three hours, starting from Davis, where she lived, through Sacramento, Stockton, Modesto, Merced and a dozen other smaller towns dotting California's fertile San Joaquin Valley. But there was little that appeared cool and refreshing along this commercial route. The areas around the cities were a mass of ugly factories and industrialized eyesores; even the orchards and farmland in between looked uninviting in Jenny's current mood. Only the shadowed peaks of the Sierra Nevada Mountains, her constant companions to the east, found any favor with her.

The episode of the aggressive truck driver who had forced her to change lanes was only one of several unpleasant encounters she had had with the huge trucks and recreational vehicles that lined the freeway. Their drivers persisted in maneuvering these outsize vehicles as if they were Alfa Romeos or Porsches, and lacked the most elemental notion of highway courtesy. After half a dozen unpleasant incidents, Jenny ached for the sight of a green and white sign indicating the exit to Fresno, and the opportunity to relax over a leisurely lunch.

She pushed her fashionably oversized sunglasses on top of her dark, ponytailed head and rubbed her eyes with the back of a weary, turquoise-and-silver ringed hand. The temperature on this early August day had already soared into the low 100's, and at first Jenny had not planned to stop at any of the restaurants lining the route. She knew that the blazing summer sun would turn the car into an oven on wheels in the time it took to drink a single glass of iced tea. But now the desire to unwind and fill her empty stomach was beginning to overrule her eagerness to reach her motel in Bakersfield.

After nearly two months of steady arguments with her father about leaving school, Jenny could hardly believe she was on her way to Scottsdale, Arizona. In fact, she thought to herself with a humorless smile, he had successfully forestalled such a trip for closer to three years than two months. Suddenly the sweetest sense of freedom washed over her, and the smile became entrancingly genuine.

Her sense of triumph was interrupted by the gleam of an aluminum-sided monster. The truck was almost parallel to her on the downward-sloping entrance ramp and Jenny caught a glimpse of it out of the right-hand window. The driver was roaring down onto the freeway as if he expected every other vehicle on the road to submissively change lanes to make way for him. Jenny abruptly decided that she had taken enough of such aggressive tactics. She kept her speed at exactly 57 miles per hour and refused to budge her car from the right-hand lane, even though the access lane ended a short distance ahead. She suffered the angry roar of the truck's horn beside her. "Serves him right!" she mumbled to herself as she heard a low groan of brakes. The next noise to assault her ears was the piercing crunch of metal against concrete as the truck driver, unable to slow his vehicle quickly enough, was forced to choose between hitting Jenny's car or scraping his truck against the high guardwall to his right. He selected the latter alternative, and a shaken Jenny accelerated sharply and continued south.

She fully expected the driver to speed up and pass

her. She was even prepared for a furious glare or obscene gesture as he did so. Indeed, several minutes later the truck appeared in her rearview mirror, but instead of passing her the driver simply followed close behind her. A series of nervous glances into the mirror identified a dark-haired figure wearing the sort of sunglasses that hid the wearer's eyes behind a silvery, reflecting mask. As the miles slid past and the driver gave no intention of passing, his presence began to rattle Jenny badly. She slowed down; he did the same. She sped up and passed several cars; he mimicked her maneuvers. Finally she decided to exit the freeway at her next opportunity, aware that she was trembling with fear at the possibility that the truck would simply trail her off the road.

She admitted to herself that she had done something not only stupid but dangerous, and cursed her hot temper for the even hotter water it had apparently landed her in. A mile later she signaled a right turn and smoothly eased into the exit lane. When the truck swung into the left-hand lane and barreled on toward the south, she found herself shaking with relief.

Half an hour later, after pulling back onto the freeway, she reached Fresno. A large blue and white sign caught her eye, the insignia on it proclaiming that the advertised motel and restaurant belonged to a well-known five-state chain. In fact, Jenny had reservations at its motor inns in Bakersfield and Indio. She knew that the chain's reputation assured her of a good meal, so she exited the freeway and doubled back underneath the overpass toward the restaurant.

As she walked in, she sighed with contentment at the welcome sight of asparagus ferns and redwood paneling. The soothing decor was very much to Jenny's liking, as were the aromas emanating from the booths adjacent to her own. Her perusal of the menu was interrupted by her awareness of a cold masculine gaze. She glanced up to see a man standing next to her table. He was wearing faded, body-hugging blue jeans and a short-sleeved tan shirt, and stared down at her with piercing blue eyes, his gaze mentally dissecting her. She brushed her ponytail from its resting spot over her left shoulder to let it fall down her back, the motion unconsciously seductive. Then she met his insulting stare with an icy one of her own. This man needed to be put in his place.

"Did you want something?" she asked coldly.

"Could be." He eased his 6'3" frame into the banquette opposite her and stretched his long legs out under the table so that they fleetingly touched hers.

Jenny jerked her feet away. "If you're looking for a cheap pickup, you're wasting your time," she informed him haughtily.

A suggestion of a smile teased the corners of his mouth. "You do yourself an injustice. You look anything but cheap."

With that sally Jenny decided that she had taken enough from this arrogant stranger. She slid over to the end of the seat and started to leave, only to be stopped dead by the man's barked out order: "Sit down, Miss Ross!"

Stunned because he knew her name, Jenny never considered disobeying. Her self-confident aloofness turned to wary uncertainty.

"How do you know who I am? What do you want?"

"You drive a 1976 blue Chevy, license plate NAJA?" he asked lazily.

She nodded. In the back of her mind was the thought

that perhaps her car was blocking his or parked illegally. He could have found her registration in the glove compartment.

"In that case," the man went on, "come with me."

His aura of command was so overpowering that Jenny found herself docilely trailing him out of the restaurant. They walked through the lobby and up half a flight of stairs leading to a wing of the building housing guest rooms. Only as he pulled a key out of his pocket did she begin to feel panicky regret that she had meekly trotted along behind him. She turned to leave, only to have her arm captured in an unrelenting grip. With his other hand he knocked on the door of one of the rooms.

A female voice called out, "Yes?" With a low curse, the man dragged a struggling Jenny to the next room. A second knock produced no response. He quickly unlocked the door, pulled Jenny into the room, and kicked the door shut with vicious impatience.

Although Jenny was badly frightened, her temper soon rose in reaction to the man's high-handed treatment.

"What do you want? What do you think you're doing?" she yelled up at him, mostly in bravado and desperation.

He ignored her questions. She was picked up and slung over his shoulder like a sailor's duffle bag. As he walked toward the bed, a terrified Jenny began to fight in earnest. She beat against his back and wriggled wildly, only to be tossed on the bed like a worn-out rag doll. When the man sat down next to her, she sat bolt upright, ready to make her escape.

But rape was very far from what he had in mind. The next instant Jenny found herself face down on the bed, pinned over his lap. "This," he said angrily, "is for this morning."

The humiliation of it was even worse than the pain. And it *was* painful. His large hand connected with her bottom six times, and even through the denim of her jeans she winced with each stinging slap. Her fierce resistance accomplished nothing. She gritted her teeth and waited for the seventh slap, only to be turned over and hauled to her feet. She backed away from him, her body stiff with fury.

The man's dark hair provided a clue to his identity. He could only be the driver of the silvery monster that Jenny had forced into an accident. Under any normal circumstances she would have been contritely apologetic. Now that her temper of the morning had cooled, she acknowledged that her actions had been inexcusable.

It was an appalling quirk of fate that the man should choose to stop at the same restaurant as she had. He must have noticed her car, then come inside in search of a ponytailed young woman dining alone. If he had calmly introduced himself to Jenny, instead of inflicting the most mortifying sort of punishment on her, she no doubt would have offered to pay for the damage.

Instead, his agressive behavior had succeeded only in enraging her. If she hadn't spent a good part of her twenty-one years in futile rebellion against her father's dominating nature, she would have informed him that her father was California Assembly Speaker Emerson Ross, Jr., a man with the connections and power to see that no trucking firm ever employed the man again. But Jenny had fought too hard for her freedom to ask her father for protection.

Her reaction was pure feminine instinct. Her right hand shot out to slap his face, only to be forced down before connecting with the intended target by a sharp karate chop to her wrist. Angrily rubbing the throbbing joint, Jenny swung on her heel, a prelude to marching out of the room. The man's hand gripped her shoulder to prevent her from leaving. Then he very deliberately turned her around to face him, his hands somehow intimate on her shoulders.

"You—you beast!" she hissed furiously. "Do you beat your wife, too?"

"Not lately," he drawled. "Anyone who plays the kinds of games you play deserves to be beaten. You're lucky I had room to stop the truck before I hit you. You could have been killed."

Under other circumstances Jenny might have admitted he was right. But his tactics had outraged her. "Me?" she sputtered. "Playing games? You were going too fast. And you tailgated me. You were trying to frighten me."

"Trying to?" he questioned dryly.

"All right, succeeded," Jenny snapped. "You were going at least 60 coming onto the freeway. I should report you to your company. You could be fired for reckless driving!"

"Be my guest. My name is Nick Butler. The company is AMT, Incorporated," he said with total unconcern.

Such lazy confidence forced her to reconsider. The man could make a convincing case that her own driving had been the cause of the accident. In any event, she decided that she had endured more than enough of the domineering Mr. Butler, if that were indeed his real name.

He seemed to read her mind. A wallet was smoothly

drawn from his rear pocket, and an Arizona driver's license flashed under her nose. It read "Nicholas Joshua Butler, Jr."

"I'm impressed," Jenny muttered sarcastically. She eyed the suntanned hand still resting on her shoulder. "If you're finished taking your revenge . . ." she said pointedly.

"Maybe," he drawled, and looked nonchalantly at the queen-size bed. "On the other hand, you owe me for the truck. And there's more than one way of paying a bill."

A wave of heat rose from Jenny's neck to her face, staining her cheeks a pale pink. The sparkle of amusement in Nick Butler's eyes told Jenny that he was only needling her; nonetheless, her body trembled with an apprehension she sought to disguise.

"What would your wife say?" she asked, in what she hoped was a crushing tone.

"She's the last one who would have minded," he informed her, his mouth twisted into a sardonic smile.

Jenny took a few steps backward, jerking her shoulder out from beneath his hand. To her relief, Nick Butler made no attempt to stop her. She turned her back to him and began a queenly march toward the door, half-expecting to feel his fingers on her body again. But as she opened the door and stepped into the hall, all she heard was the sound of laughter.

Jenny's first instinct was to flee the restaurant, putting as much distance as possible between herself and Nick Butler. But she was as stubborn as she was hot-tempered and nothing would make her bolt in the face of his aggression. She would eat the leisurely lunch she had promised herself, even if she had to force down every bite, then drive the last hour to Bakersfield.

She ordered a salad of fresh fruit with marshmallow sauce, and the sight of the beautifully arranged platter soon restored her appetite. Every so often she would glimpse a tall, dark figure out of the corner of her eye and the hairs on the back of her neck would prickle, but none of these other diners turned out to be Nick Butler. As she ate, she resolutely pushed aside all thoughts of the arrogant truck driver, trying instead to concentrate on the job that awaited her in Scottsdale.

But when she returned to her car and started south, she found herself brooding about much of what had happened. After the accident, she had left the freeway and waited for several minutes before continuing, ample time for Nick Butler to gain a substantial lead on her. Yet he had apparently arrived at the restaurant after she had. She concluded that he must have stopped, perhaps for gas.

More bewildering was an incident that Jenny thought of only in retrospect. The truck driver had knocked on a motel room door, found that someone was in the room, and proceeded to the next room down the hall. Presumably he had checked in for the night, perhaps stopping early due to the damage to the truck. But surely he would know his room number—it would be on the key.

Jenny gave an abrupt shake of her head. It made no sense. A suspicious frown crossed her face at the thought that Nick Butler was somehow connected with her father. She didn't put it past Emerson Ross to hire someone to follow her down to Scottsdale. But Jenny rejected the notion that her urbane father would hire a truck driver like Nick Butler to play private eye. Ultimately she abandoned her attempt to analyze what she hoped would turn out to be an isolated, if extremely unpleasant, incident.

She emerged from her car in Bakersfield, only to be greeted by a blast of heat, and was so weary that the five minutes she stood and waited her turn at the registration desk seemed like fifteen. But soon she was pulling her car to the rear of one of the motel's three buildings, easily following the polite directions of the reservation clerk. She carried a small overnight case into the spacious, attractively decorated room, leaving the rest of her luggage in the car's large trunk.

The double bed beckoned, but Jenny lay on it only five minutes before jumping up, efficiently stripping off her jeans and t-shirt, and slipping into a brown and white cotton bikini and matching terry cover-up. The outfit accentuated the dusky tan Jenny had acquired in her parents' backyard pool.

A teenager's portable radio sat on a white wrought iron table by the side of the motel pool, the disc jockey announcing between fast-paced patter that the temperature in downtown Bakersfield was 108°. Jenny could feel every degree of it. She dove gracefully into the cooling water, and swam a moderate-paced freestyle stroke several times up and down the length of the pool. When she emerged to settle in a lounge chair, the air appeared to be no more than pleasantly warm.

The owner of the radio was a young man whom Jenny judged to be about seventeen. He did not bother to be furtive in the admiring stares he bestowed on her supine body, but he made no attempt to talk to her. If he had tried, Jenny would have put him in his place without difficulty. In her twenty-one years she had found it necessary to learn to handle unwelcome displays of masculine admiration.

Jenny's maternal grandmother had bequeathed her a face that was indefinably exotic. It was impossible for a casual observer to know if her silky curtain of dark brown hair; slightly rounded, almost black eyes; straight nose; high cheekbones and full mouth were the result of Asian, Pacific Island or Native American ancestry. In fact, Jenny's grandmother had been a mixture of Navajo, Pueblo and Spanish. Her name had been Silver Moon and she had married a man named Charles Cooper, who came from a family of traders in Santa Fe. The Coopers made a handsome profit on the jewelry produced by Silver Moon's father, one of the foremost Navajo silversmiths of his day.

Although the Coopers objected to the marriage, their disapproval was mitigated by another of Silver Moon's relatives. She was the granddaughter of a tribal leader and head chief named Manuelito, who had been acclaimed for his skill and wisdom as a leader. This connection enabled the Coopers to claim, albeit inaccurately, that Silver Moon was actually an Indian princess.

Jenny considered herself a throwback to her beautiful, dignified grandmother and proud and talented great-grandfather. Certainly she didn't belong with her father's haughtily partrician family. She felt quite out of place when she visited the old-line law firm where Emerson Ross, Sr. was a partner, or attended parties at the San Francisco townhouse where her paternal grandmother entertained the social, political and commercial leaders of the city. If she endured these functions with good grace, it was because she hoped that if she behaved properly, her father would permit her some independence. Although she was rebellious, she had no desire to alienate her parents.

After a final dip in the pool, Jenny strolled back to her room. She changed into a knee-length cotton robe and lay down on the bed to read, dozing off in the middle of an extremely boring chapter of a long historical novel she was determined to finish. She woke up two hours later, ready for dinner. After dressing in a casual navy and white pantsuit she made her way across the pool and patio area through a back door into the motor inn's restaurant, catching the eye of the hostess, who seated her at a small, quiet table along a wall.

As she sipped a glass of white wine and waited for her scampi to arrive, her mind skipped unbidden to her last, icy argument with her parents. Once the academic year ended, Jenny had insisted that she wanted to leave school and her parents' home. Her father had been just as insistent that she had no job waiting for her and no preparation for a career. He brushed aside her considerable skill as a silversmith, calling it a mere schoolgirl's hobby, ridiculing the notion that Jenny might have inherited some of her great-grandfather's talent. He refused to help support her until she could make a living selling her jewelry.

Then, only three weeks ago, her friend Sheila Werner had mentioned that her father's cousin and his wife needed a mother's helper/housekeeper to take care of their nine year old granddaughter. The couple lived in the city of Scottsdale, Arizona, near Phoenix. To Jenny, it was as though a personal guardian angel had arranged the opportunity for her special benefit. The Arizona area was a prime market for the type of jewelry she crafted and a job caring for a nine year old could not possibly take up all of her time, nor would she need her father's help or a degree to get it.

In order to learn more, she asked Sheila to invite her to dinner and soon she was questioning Mr. Werner as to her suitability for the position. At first he was skeptical, he knew she was only halfway through college. But he listened to her arguments and found them persuasive. One long-distance phone call later the matter was arranged—providing that Jenny could obtain her father's approval.

Jenny felt strongly that now that she was twenty-one years old she shouldn't need her father's permission for anything. But she understood that Jonathan Werner had no wish to antagonize her father. State Assemblyman Emerson Ross had represented the wealthy area around Pebble Beach for over a decade. As Speaker of the Assembly for the past six years, he was the second most powerful man in California politics, right after the Governor; not many people wanted to land themselves on his blacklist. Especially not a man like Mr. Werner, who happened to make his living as a lobbyist for a number of small industries in the state.

At first Jenny's father had flatly refused to consider allowing her to leave home. Jacqueline Ross, as usual, sided with her forceful husband. Jenny, as always hot-tempered in response to her father's domination, was absolutely livid with rage. But she kept her sarcastic tongue frosty as she informed him that she had a right to live her own life and make her own mistakes. She pointed out that she had eschewed the permissive attitudes toward sex and experimentation with drugs embraced by so many of her peers. Yet, she said frigidly, her maturity and responsibility had not earned her her parents' trust. She threatened to leave with or without their permission and with or without a job.

Her arguments, whether uttered in a tone of utmost rationality or shrieked in a voice of uncontained fury, were met by stony refusal. And Jonathan Werner's cousin would not consider hiring Jenny without her father's approval. Jenny started looking for an apartment in Sacramento. She had been determined to secure her father's permission and his blessing, but she began to feel that it would be impossible.

Then, a week and a half ago, Emerson Ross had returned from his office and favored his daughter with a measured smile. He had reconsidered, he announced, and decided that Jenny was free to go to Scottsdale. He made only two conditions: he would make her motel reservations for her, and she was not to leave until the following week. Jenny happily agreed.

The Valley Motor Inn was part of a chain known for excellent conference facilities, quiet, attractive rooms and good food. As Jenny nibbled on a shrimp, she was forced to approve her father's choice. After dinner, she walked into the lobby on her way to the sundries shop for a paperback or magazine to read that evening. A large billboard caught her eye; the sign announced that a four-piece combo would be playing from nine o'clock until midnight. Jenny adored music and dancing, and it took her only a few seconds to abandon any thoughts of a quiet evening. Besides, she needed some casual amusement to prevent her from brooding about her earlier misadventure. She thought guiltily that this afternoon she had justified her father's worst opinion of her, and prayed that he never got wind of the episode.

Back in her room, she showered, washed and dried

her hair, and donned a street-length, halter-topped sundress splashed with turquoise, blue and green. She hesitated before adding the jewelry that she always wore with the dress—it might be too fancy for Bakersfield, she thought. Then she shrugged and fastened it about her neck.

It was a stunning silver and turquoise choker, the work the finest Jenny had ever seen. She had received it as a twenty-first birthday present from her father. She knew it was ungracious of her to persistently assign the lowest of motives to Emerson Ross, but nonetheless, she could not escape the feeling that he had presented it to her as a subtle comment on her own talents. Jenny was aware that she could only aspire to the excellence of the Zuni master craftsman who had designed and created the necklace. Her own delicate silver jewelry was beautiful, but she would need a good deal more practice before she would be able to even approximate the exquisite craftsmanship of the necklace she wore. But she was determined that nothing would stop her from trying.

Once seated in the lounge, she ordered a strawberry daiquiri and listened as the combo swung into a medley of hit movie themes. Jenny loved dancing and was extremely good at it, and when she saw her seventeen year old admirer from the pool looking boldly over at her, she decided to encourage him. She smiled warmly. The young man's macho swagger appeared to fail him. He blushed and looked down, then hesitatingly made his way over to her and asked her to dance. Jenny's twinkling "I thought you'd never ask" was a boost to his confidence. The band began a pulse-quickening rock number to which Jenny and her partner did full justice. Hands flung out, bodies moving with liquid grace, feet easily mimicking the latest intricate steps, they were soon giving an exhibition to an appreciative audience. Jenny had never expected Bakersfield to be so much fun, and as she and her partner danced to song after song, she knew she was delighted she had decided to come to the lounge tonight.

Until she saw *him*. In the back of her mind there had been the niggling fear that she would encounter Nick Butler again. Although there was no logic in the feeling, since the man was apparently registered at a motel in Fresno, somehow Jenny was more dismayed than shocked. She retreated to her seat and ordered a second strawberry daiquiri; she needed something to help her stomach the presence of the dominating Mr. Butler.

She watched him out of the corner of one wary eye. He stopped the waitress and spoke to her, presumably ordering a drink. Then he walked over to the band, had a few words with the lead musician, and coolly strolled over to the couch where Jenny was sitting. The waitress had just brought her drink and, strangely, she tasted no rum at all.

"You're a good dancer."

Jenny stared stonily at her drink and made no reply. She could do without his compliments.

He sat down next to her, sipping an amber liquid, thoroughly at ease. Jenny, her body rigid with dislike, refused to give him the satisfaction of running away. She ignored him.

When the band finished yet another frenetic number, he leaned over and whispered in her ear, "Dance with me."

Jenny produced the most scornful look she was capable of mustering and said sarcastically, "You don't look like the acid rock type to me. You're much too old."

His eyes glowed with amusement. "That's really hitting below the belt, Jenny. Especially since I'm only thirty-three. But I told them to play something slow."

The man's presumption was appalling. He *told* them, not asked them, Jenny thought to herself, and snapped, "For a truck driver, you sure have a lot of nerve. Do you always order people around?"

"Always," he agreed solemnly. He calmly removed the drink from her hand and set it down on the end table along with his own. Then he firmly took hold of her wrist and rose, pulling her up with him.

Although sorely provoked, Jenny had no wish to make a scene. She allowed herself to be led to the center of the room and stoically endured his loose hold on her body. The band began a slow, soulful number. Nick pulled her closer until his chin was resting against her hair. One hand caressed her bare back, then dropped lower and splayed itself across the base of her spine, pressing her body intimately against his. The fingers of his other hand crept under her thick, silky hair to grasp the nape of her neck, his thumb absent-mindedly massaging the sensitive area under her right ear.

Jenny tried desperately to ignore the effect this was having on her. There was no point in denying that the man was a superb male specimen. His longish dark hair and piercing blue eyes made him look vaguely satanic, as did his cleft-chinned jaw and thin-lipped mouth, which Jenny doubted was capable of a smile. Held close against him, she could feel the muscles in his arms and chest and thighs, and decided that he must spend as much time exercising as driving a truck. There was no softness in him, only hard, demanding strength.

But as handsome as he might be, Jenny told herself that he was also an arrogant beast. She held her body as tautly as she could manage. Then his left hand abandoned its hold on her back to move further around her body and lightly caress her hip. Jenny tried to wiggle away, hissing angrily, "Stop it!"

"Stop what?" he whispered, his lips brushing against her hair, his hand stroking her side.

Jenny said nothing, choosing instead to very deliberately grind the spike of her sandal into his booted foot. Her partner only laughed softly, nipped her ear with calculated sensuousness and drawled, "I may bite, Jenny, but I promise not to seduce you here in the middle of the dance floor."

"You flatter yourself," she said sourly.

The band was drawing out the final chord of the song. Nick put Jenny away from him and gently slipped a finger under her chin to tilt it up. He studied her outraged expression. "Perhaps," he mocked. "Would you care to make a bet on that?"

It was all but impossible for Jenny to turn up her nose at someone a good foot taller than her own 5′3″, but she made a valiant stab at it. She shrugged out of his arms, tossed her hair, and stalked back to her seat. Thereafter, she studiously ignored the presence of Nick Butler.

During the next hour she danced with a variety of partners, angrily aware, despite herself, that Nick was sprawled in a chair at the opposite end of the room, keeping a sardonic eye on her every action. For the second time that day she had a strong urge to go over and inform him that her father was Assemblyman Emerson Ross, Jr., thank you very much, and if Nicholas Butler knew what was good for him, he would leave her alone.

But it would have been simply too galling to have to use as a weapon the clout she had claimed to hate for the past five or six years. It infuriated Jenny that she had delivered setdowns to men far more sophisticated than Nick Butler, who after all was only a truck driver. He had probably grown up in some hick town in Arizona, yet she was finding him impossible to handle.

No doubt the man's objectionable over-confidence stemmed from his looks. Jenny thought moodily that he was probably used to having women fall all over him. No doubt he had an unsuspecting wife and family tucked away somewhere, blissfully unaware of his activities. He seemed to feel free to amuse himself on his travels with whomever he decided to honor with his attention.

Jenny glanced at her watch. It was 11:00—surely late enough that Nick Butler couldn't accuse her of running away from him. As she made her way to the door, she was aware of Nick's eyes following her progress. But he made no move to get up.

Jenny was halfway across the pool area before she realized that there was someone behind her. Suddenly apprehensive, she increased her pace, her body jerking violently when she felt a heavy hand squeeze her shoulder.

"Relax," Nick Butler told her evenly, "I just want to make sure you get back to your room all right."

His presumption goaded Jenny to visions of revenge. She spun around to face him, dearly wishing she had the strength to push him in the pool. "Since when did you turn into my protector?" she sputtered, her temper only marginally under control.

"Someone has to be. After that exhibition on the dance floor, you're lucky you don't have every unattached male over the age of sixteen trying to climb in your window. And half the married ones, too."

Jenny's hands flew to her hips in a gesture of outraged protest. "*You're* the only one I have to worry about! You'd better leave me alone, Mr. Butler, because if you so much as touch me again, I'll scream the place down!"

Her threat only amused him. "No you won't," he said laconically. "Now be a good girl and come back to your room."

Jenny, more enraged than she could remember feeling in all her volatile years, choked back the unladylike curse she ached to spit at him and began a stiff-backed retreat to her room. As she inserted the key into the lock, Nick Butler leaned against the building, patiently watching her.

She all but kicked the door open. "Good-night, *Mr.* Butler," she said frigidly, "and good riddance." She tried to slam the door in his face, telling herself that her accelerated heartbeats were due only to anger, and certainly not to fear or arousal.

A well-muscled arm forced the door wide open. "Not quite," Nicholas Butler announced, following Jenny into her room. "Kiss me good-night first."

"You have *got* to be kidding," Jenny said, rolling her eyes. "You're the most arrogant, chauvinistic man I've ever met. I'd kiss a snake before I'd kiss you!"

Nick nodded. "I see. And here I was congratulating myself at my good luck in—uh—running into you again. Still angry with me for walloping you, hmm?"

Nick was refusing to take her objections seriously, and Jenny's anger threatened to escalate into total incoherence. She clenched her fists at her sides and accused, "You're—you're following me."

"I'm going to Tucson. I'll probably get there late tomorrow," Nick informed her.

"You had—you had a room in Fresno," Jenny charged, "and then you came here."

"Two rooms, which belonged to a friend I happened to run into outside the restaurant." He winked at the outraged Jenny. "Unluckily for you. I would never have spanked you in public, even though you deserved it."

Jenny decided that she had wasted too much time with this conceited man. Her tone was icily nasty as she told him, "Send me your address and the bill. I'll be at the Oscar Hermann residence in Scottsdale—you can check the phone book for the address. Now get out of here before I call the security guard."

Nick only smiled, closed the door behind them, and cocked his head toward the phone. "Go ahead," he invited. "Just dial 4 and ask the desk to send him around."

Jenny eyed him suspiciously. "Why don't you care? Did you pay him off or something?"

"Or something." He put out a hand to gently smooth her hair, and the feel of his fingers was dangerously exciting. The next moment a struggling Jenny was being pulled into his arms, her hair caught and twined around the fingers of one strong hand, her arms caught behind her back by the second. Although Jenny forced herself to stand rigidly in his arms, his closeness was swamping her senses with a mindless desire to respond. A quick glance at the grin on his face confirmed that he knew perfectly well the effect he was having on her, but Jenny told herself she would prove to him that she was no easy mark. Eventually he would try to kiss her, and when he did, she would see to it that he was very, very sorry.

But Nick simply tipped her chin up, gazing into her partially-lidded dark eyes, his mouth still quirking with a smile. He held her chin firmly as he allowed his index finger to trail over her face and lips. "It's a shame," he sighed, "that I'm so honorable."

He lowered his head to lightly brush his mouth against her, and Jenny shuddered with arousal. She was acutely disappointed when Nick released her and smiled lazily down at her. "I'm supposed to be protecting you," he drawled, "not seducing you."

Jenny was totally bewildered by the comment. "What are you talking about?" she whispered.

Nick only shook his head. "Nothing. You're obviously very innocent, Jenny. Now go to bed—alone." He turned his back to her and strolled out of her room.

Jenny watched the door close, her face stained pink with embarrassment. How could she have let a virtual stranger take such liberties? She must have been insane to forget how vulnerable she was, alone in a motel room with him. After twenty-one careful, sensible years, she had practically allowed herself to be picked up like a common streetwalker! What on earth would her father think if he found out?

But thankfully, he wouldn't. Or would he? She walked over to the door to slip the chain lock into place, then dropped into a chair to think.

Nick Butler puzzled her. The events of the day puzzled her. It was stretching coincidence too far to believe that he had turned up at this motel due to some bizarre quirk of fate. Had he somehow followed her, first to the restaurant and then to Bakersfield? She certainly had not noticed his truck behind her again, but then it looked like many others on the crowded highway. The accident might have been a coincidence, but it seemed impossible that everything else was also pure chance.

Nick's suave self-assurance and sophisticated approach did not gibe with her image of the average hard-working truck driver. And then there was all that only half-humorous talk about protecting her.

Her previous suspicions reasserted themselves. Nothing about today's pulse-elevating adventures was accidental. Emerson Ross must have hired Nick Butler to keep an eye on her. The more Jenny sat and pondered Nick Butler's unusual behavior, the more convinced she became that he was some sort of private eye engaged by her father to make sure she behaved herself en route to Scottsdale. The physical attraction between them had been real, there was no doubt about that. And in spite of his sighing claim to the contrary, Nick did not strike Jenny as particularly honorable. But he was not so demented as to seduce the daughter of his powerful employer, either.

As she undressed and washed up before climbing into bed, Jenny's temper began a slow simmer. Her initial feeling that she would run into Mr. Butler in Indio tomorrow became a certainty. And when she did, she would demand some answers!

Chapter Two

The dining room of the Valley Motor Inn was too formal for Jenny's impatient mood the next morning. Besides, she had no desire to meet up with Nick Butler just yet. In their encounters of the previous day, he had easily bested her, and Jenny told herself that her defeats were the result of being taken by surprise. Now that she knew what an arrogant, lying creature he was, she wouldn't make that mistake again.

She stopped at a roadside diner, ordering a cup of tea and a large Danish and taking them back to her car to eat. The outside temperature was already approaching 90° and Jenny was grateful for the efficiency of the car's air-conditioner. As she headed southeast, toward the desert, irrigated crops gave way to ranches. Cows grazed stolidly in the rolling green fields that Jenny knew would be brown if not for the sprinklers which periodically sprayed water over the grass.

A roadrunner, like all of his species perpetually in a hurry, skittered across the pavement. Jenny was driving through high desert now; the landscape was dotted with grayish-green scrub. Mountain peaks, some still capped with snow from the previous winter's heavy precipitation, loomed all around her as she traversed mile after mile of hilly countryside. But once in the Mojave Desert the drive was hardly boring because Jenny found herself totally captivated by the Joshua trees that grew in the American southwest and in the Holy Land, but nowhere else on earth.

They stood silhouetted against the blue-white sky, sometimes in groups of three or four, sometimes alone. Each tree was unique looking, an individual. An occasional specimen reached a height of thirty-five feet or more, its many branches covered with spindly vegetation of a washed-out shade of green. Other trees had only two or three branches. There was a lonely dignity to these plants, some of which had been on the earth for over a millenium. And somehow the most stunted, distorted trees were the most affecting of all, as if they were engaged in a battle against nature for survival, and had triumphed.

Jenny chided herself for such fanciful notions until she passed a charred, fire-blackened area. The ground was scorched, the scrub dead. But in the middle of this devastation stood the Joshua trees, still alive and growing.

To Jenny's disgust, every time she spotted a silver-colored truck, her heartbeats came faster and her palms began to sweat. But none of them had AMT slashed boldly across their silver sides. She began to think that her imagination had been much too creative last night. She would never see Nick Butler again.

Perhaps he had been ahead of schedule and just amused enough by her outraged reaction to his heavy-handed revenge to follow her to Bakersfield and force her into the mortifying position of responding to his unwelcome caresses.

Her undeniable arousal at the feel of Nick's mouth and body and hands was something that Jenny was trying to forget. Last night she had been too preoccupied by the thought that he was working for her father to dwell on her reaction to his lovemaking. But this morning, during her drive through the desert, she had ample time to recall the sensations he had aroused. Never in her life had she experienced such an overpowering physical attraction to a man. How could she possibly have permitted herself to respond to a Lothario truck driver who had probably perfected his technique from San Diego to Seattle?

The desert highway intersected with a multi-lane freeway as Jenny approached sprawling San Bernardino, which was close enough to Los Angeles to be on the fringes of its urban influence. The eerie beauty of the desert seemed far away from this heavily developed area of the state. Jenny had long ago finished her Danish and was now hungry, but her eagerness to reach Indio was stronger than the complaints of her stomach. The last hour and a half was traveled southeast on an excellent freeway but Jenny found the drive tedious in spite of the often striking mountain vistas. She longed for the sight of trees and grass, not this brown, sparsely vegetated terrain.

The Date Garden Motor Inn was another link in the chain that included the Valley Motor Inn. Jenny's legs were rubbery as she staggered out of the car and endured the familiar blast of desert heat. She checked in and drove her car to her room, much too hungry to do more than throw her small suitcase on the bed.

Once seated in the blissfully cool restaurant, she ordered a chef's salad, correctly assuming that it would come more quickly than anything else on the menu. The waitress took in her exhausted face and instantly brought the iced tea she had requested. It felt wonderfully refreshing after those brief moments outside. A huge salad and warm biscuits soon followed, and Jenny managed to eat two-thirds of the crisp, fresh produce before she set down her fork in defeat.

Later, having unpacked her suitcase, she slithered into her bikini and spent the afternoon by the pool. The water was tepid, like a giant bathtub, and more enervating than refreshing. But once she got out and lay down on a shaded lounge chair to let the breeze play over her wet skin, she felt completely comfortable in spite of the desert heat.

The pool was located to the side of the extensive motel grounds, hidden from the main building by a chain fence and surrounding shrubs. As she emerged from the pool area Jenny instinctively glanced around the parking lot in search of Nick Butler's truck. She strolled along the shaded path back to her room, chagrined that she should feel disappointment at its absence. Of course, she told herself, the letdown she had experienced was due only to the fact that she longed to confront the man with her accusations. It could not possibly have anything to do with wanting to see him again. She had no use for domineering, egotistical male chauvinists.

Jenny had just stepped out of a bracingly cold shower when she heard a loud knock on the door. As she wrapped a large orange towel around her dripping body, she emerged from the bathroom to call out warily, "Yes? Who is it?"

An instantly recognized masculine voice answered, "It's Nick. Let me in."

Jenny's blood pressure rose ten percent—from anger, she insisted to herself. "Go away," she ordered. "I'm not dressed."

A soft laugh. "I don't mind. C'mon, Jenny. It's hot as hell out here." The soft coaxing tone of his voice had a devastating effect on Jenny's equilibrium.

She was standing in the middle of the room, rooted to the carpet in indecision, when the knob of the door began to turn. She stared at it—she was certain she had locked it. She quickly walked to the closet to retrieve her light cotton wrap.

Nick walked in as she was putting her right arm through the sleeve. "I prefer the towel," he chuckled, and then stretched out on her bed.

Jenny fished some clothing from the dresser and stalked off into the bathroom. She told herself that she was extremely annoyed with the man. After all, he was supposed to be on his way to Tucson. But since he *had* shown up, she was going to discover his reason for following her around. Jeans and a sleeveless shell were hastily jerked on. Jenny grabbed her brush and opened the door to confront him.

As she brusquely tugged the brush through her tangled, wet hair, she accused, "This can't possibly be another coincidence. What are you doing here? I thought you were on your way to Tucson."

Nick yawned, entirely at home on her bed. "I had some trouble with the truck so I decided to stop for the night." His smile was teasing. "Aren't you pleased that I decided to surprise you?"

Jenny bit back the acid reply she longed to fling at him. Losing her temper would accomplish nothing.

"Admit it, Jenny," Nick continued seductively. "Last night you would have eagerly—"

Sorely goaded, Jenny interrupted furiously, "Last night I was out of my mind! Don't let it give you any ideas." Then, determined to trap him into admitting his connection with her father, she went on, "I don't suppose you checked every motel in Palm Springs and Indio. How did you know where I'd be?"

"Reasonable deduction," he drawled. "You were heading toward Phoenix and this belongs to the same chain as the Valley Motor Inn. While the truck was being fixed, I called up to check whether you had a reservation."

"How did you get into my room?" she snapped, not believing his answer but unable to challenge the logic of it.

"It was open. You should be more careful." His tone was scolding, his face now perfectly solemn.

Since yelling had accomplished nothing, Jenny decided to try flattery. "Gee Nick, you know you don't really seem like the truck driver type. You're much too sophisticated. Who are you, really?"

His face lit up with amusement as he stretched and swung his legs over the side of the bed. "You know I'm not going to answer your questions. I came to take you over to dinner. The restaurant here is as good as any in town. Hungry?"

"My father hired you, didn't he?" Jenny persisted.

"Absolutely not," Nick said firmly. "I promise you, nobody's paying me to tail you. You underestimate yourself."

For the first time, Jenny permitted the look on her

face to soften from suspicion and dislike to neutral blandness. She didn't know why, but she believed his last statement. Still, even if her father weren't paying him, there might be some other connection. "You've never met my father, then? You don't owe him any favors?"

Nick shook his head. "Nope." He lifted himself from the bed and walked to within a yard of where Jenny was standing, the tousled state of her hair now forgotten. His nearness was more intoxicating than half a dozen strawberry daiquiris and she had a shattering urge to reach out and touch him. One look into his intense blue eyes and she stopped resisting it.

She took a step toward him and lifted her hand to trail it along his bristly jaw; Nick seized her errant fingers and turned her hand over to nuzzle her palm. "Not now, Jenny," he told her quietly. "I want to shower and change. I'll meet you in the dining room in half an hour."

He pressed a hard kiss into her still imprisoned palm, released her hand and, without another word, let himself out of the room.

Jenny stared at the closed door, feeling bewildered and off-balance. Did his soft "Not now" imply that later . . . ? And if it did, what was she going to do about it? What did she want? Certainly not a one-night affair in some stranger's motel room. Yet if Nick were after only that, he might well have accomplished his objective last night. Perhaps she was no more than a source of casual amusement during a boring trip. Or perhaps he was lying through his teeth and was indeed on Emerson Ross's payroll.

With a sigh, Jenny told herself that none of it made any sense and no amount of speculation would produce a logical explanation. During dinner, she would wait for a subtle opportunity to question him. She picked up her brush and blow dryer; soon her hair was a smooth, silky mass. Then she slipped on a casual green and white striped sundress and walked over to the dining room. It was only 6:30 and few people were eating dinner yet. Nick was not in the restaurant, so Jenny mentioned to the hostess that she was waiting for someone who would probably be joining her in a little while. The woman looked at Jenny appraisingly, then smiled. "Let's see how my intuition is today. You're waiting for Mr. Butler, am I right?"

There was something curious about the way she said "Mr. Butler." Respectful. Even slightly awestruck. Jenny decided some subtle pumping was in order, and she would never have a better opening.

She nodded. "We met by the pool. Tell me, does he stay here often?" Her tone was casual to the point of indifference.

"Indio isn't exactly the crossroads of the state," the hostess smiled. "I see him here a few times a year, on business. You know—to check up on things." She looked sheepish. "Frankly, when we hear he's coming we really spiff things up. It wouldn't do to have the place less than perfect when the boss shows up. But this trip he surprised us."

"Boss?" Jenny sputtered.

"You don't know much about him, do you?" the hostess asked. "He's the president of the corporation, so I guess that makes him the boss, doesn't it?"

Jenny was momentarily stunned. Her face reddening with anger at the magnitude of the man's deception, she asked in a strangled voice, "He *owns* this motel?"

The hostess was obviously amused by Jenny's ignorance. "Of course. The whole chain. But he's awfully nice and down-to-earth." She escorted Jenny to an intimate table in a quiet corner of the room. "Can I get you a drink?"

Jenny knew she would need to keep her wits about her tonight—no strawberry daiquiris this evening, and certainly nothing stronger. "Just iced tea, please," she told the waitress, who hurried away to fill her order. Obviously out to please the boss, Jenny thought grimly. Well, "the boss" was going to get his comeuppance tonight.

An unsuspecting Nick Butler was greeted by Jenny's stormy countenance as he approached the table. She had considered simply leaving, perhaps scrawling a sarcastic note on the cloth napkin in explanation. But she was spoiling for a fight, and she was going to see that he knew it.

"Well, if it isn't the tycoon of the Far West," Jenny fumed as soon as he was seated. She stared across the table at him, her expression tight-lipped and challenging.

"Ah," he said with laughter in his eyes, "my secret identity has been uncovered. How did you find out?"

"*Your* hostess told me," Jenny replied icily. "She seems to think you're one step down from Albert Schweitzer."

"Good for my ego." He eyed her empty glass. "Off the strawberry daiquiris, Jenny?" he teased.

"They were too weak for my taste anyway. My only complaint about *your* motel, except for its owner."

"I told the bartender to go easy on the rum. The second drink had no liquor at all in it," Nick informed her airily. At her enraged reaction to this blithe admission, he gibed, "What are you so steamed up about, Jenny? I'm not a private detective, am I?"

"Who knows what else you are!" Jenny snapped.

"We own the trucking company," he laughed. "Also date orchards and processing plants, citrus groves in California and Arizona, an interest in copper and molybdenum mines, real estate, a casino in Vegas and a few other odds and ends."

"I'm so impressed," Jenny said acidly. "I hoped you've enjoyed your little game."

"Thoroughly, or else I wouldn't have bothered to keep playing it, Jenny. Now stop pouting and let's have dinner. The prime rib is excellent here."

"And you should know, shouldn't you?" Jenny shot back sarcastically. "Tell me, do you own the ranch the steer came from, too?"

Nick roared with laughter. "No, I'm not into ranching. Yet." A nod of his head instantly summoned the waitress; he proceeded to order for both of them. Then he coaxed, "Tell me about yourself, Jenny. Why are you going to Scottsdale?"

"Don't you know?" Jenny glared at him, her temper simmering.

Nick Butler's lips twitched, his half-smiling expression wholly engaging. "Jenny!" he admonished. "I have access to our reservations system. It was no problem to find out where you'd be tonight, since you prepaid for a room here. And it was a good opportunity for me to check up on a few business dealings. I told you I was going to Tucson because I knew that temper of yours would explode when I turned up, and I couldn't deprive myself of that pleasure." He winked at her. "You're beautiful when you're angry. Which is probably just as well, because you seem to be in a perpetual state of pique.''

Jenny flung her napkin onto the table and glowered at him, ready to stalk out of the room.

"You know I'll only follow you and bring you back here,'' Nick informed her cheerfully, his whole manner warm and teasing. "Where's your sense of humor, Jenny?'' He began to laugh again.

Jenny never knew exactly when her anger turned to mirth. One moment she was rising from her chair, meeting his eyes with sparks of fury shooting out of her own. Then, somehow, she made the mistake of allowing herself to be captivated by his smile, and the next moment she was laughing along with him. With a rueful shrug, she sat down again.

"You certainly have a unique approach, Mr. Butler,'' she said dryly. "First spanking the dickens out of me—''

"Which you thoroughly deserved,'' he cut in.

"And then, well . . .'' Jenny's voice trailed off, her cheeks heating up as she remembered how easily this man could arouse her. She abruptly changed the subject back to Nick Butler. "So you're really a millionaire, bored with life, in search of a little diversion, right?''

"Something like that,'' Nick agreed. "I did follow you to the restaurant, and then to Bakersfield. I'm surprised you didn't notice the truck.''

Nick's reference to his mode of transportation made Jenny suspicious all over again. "How come you're driving a truck, anyway?'' she demanded. "How do I know that you're not really a truck driver who paid off the hostess?''

"What a devious mind you have!" Nick interrupted. "The truck's a prototype,—I wanted to test drive it myself before I purchased a fleet for the business." He contrived to look wounded at Jenny's skeptical expression. "Here I've come clean about my nefarious activities and you don't believe me. Okay, Exhibit A. I was looking for a vacant room in Fresno to haul you into. The first one I tried was occupied. The next one down the hall was empty; I used a master key to get in. Exhibit B. I didn't care if you called the security guard, because he would have taken one look at me and said, 'Is everything all right, Mr. Butler?' and gone on his way. And Exhibit C. I let myself into your locked room today. Satisfied?"

"You're trying to rile me again," Jenny accused.

"Not at all. I'm giving you an explanation. Isn't that what you wanted?" Nick asked innocently.

"Oh all right!" Jenny conceded. "Just so long as you understand that I'm not a total idiot who believes everything you tell me. Where are you really going?"

"I told you, Tucson, on business. Now tell me why you're going to Scottsdale."

The waitress arrived with Nick's drink, which he sipped while waiting for Jenny's reply. Everything he had told her fit into place, and she really had no further excuse to be irritated with him. In fact, it was rather flattering that a man of Nick Butler's wealth and obvious charm should choose to trail her down half the state of California. There was no reason not to answer his question.

"I have a job there, as sort of a mother's helper and housekeeper. The main reason I want to go to Arizona is because I make Indian-type jewelry and it's the center of the market."

Nick nodded. "The necklace you were wearing last night—did you—?"

"I wish I had," Jenny said with a wistful smile. "My father gave it to me. It's Zuni and I do Navajo-type work, mostly in silver with no stones."

"That's where your unusual looks come from? You're part Indian?"

"Yes. My grandmother was mostly Navajo," Jenny told him, not displeased by his apparent fascination with her face. "She married a white trader. Her father was one of the most famous silversmiths of his time, and her grandfather was a head chief. Grandma died six years ago, but she told me that when my mother was a little girl, her greatest ambition was to become a lawyer and help her people. She met my father in law school, dropped out to marry him, and now she's just like his whole family. Old-line and proper."

Nick's eyebrows arched in inquiry. "You've mentioned your father several times. Is he someone I should have heard of?"

"The honorable Emerson Ross, Jr., Speaker of the Assembly of the State of California," Jenny said sarcastically. "You do business in the Golden State. Surely you employ one of the lobbyists who are always swarming around him?"

"The associations we belong to do," Nick agreed. "But why so negative about him? He's got a reputation for honesty and competence. Is it undeserved?"

"Oh, no!" Jenny hastily assured him. Not once in her life had she doubted her father's integrity. "He's admirable in his public servant incarnation. But he doesn't let me run my life the way I want to. I've been making jewelry since I was ten years old. For as long as I can remember, that's how I've wanted to earn a living. After high school, Daddy decided that my refusal to go to college was due to some sort of immaturity, so he demanded that I work 'in the real world,' as he put it, for a year. He got me a job in the legislature, and it seemed more sensible to go along with him. I thought he would be satisfied once my sentence had been served, but he wasn't. I wasted two more years of my time in college, thanks to him. I'm not stupid or ignorant, Nick, but I don't care for formalized study. I know how to read and I like to learn things on my own. When the opportunity in Scottsdale came up, I was determined to go."

"And here you are."

"And here I am," Jenny agreed. The waitress had placed their meals on the table and for a time they ate in silence. Jenny realized that although Nick had reeled off a list of his assets, she really knew almost nothing else about him. He had never denied having a wife, and Jenny knew she would be wise to find out his marital status before she succumbed completely to his appeal. There was no point tiptoeing around the question, so she asked bluntly, "Are you married?"

"You have one terrific opinion of me, don't you?" Nick sipped some wine and replied coolly, "I *was* married. My wife's dead. Satisfied?"

Jenny paled with embarrassment. "Oh, Nick, I'm sorry, I didn't—"

"Don't be," he cut in harshly. "She was a tramp."

His words were so forbidding that Jenny was afraid to ask him anything else. And then he was questioning her again. "You know," he said, between bites of prime rib, "I've always wondered why your father hasn't run for higher office. Your grandfather's a senior partner in a San Francisco law firm, isn't he? With all the right financial connections?"

"That's right. But Dad honestly feels he's making a valuable contribution in the legislature. He may be overbearing, but at least he's not obnoxiously ambitious."

"But he would make a fine governor, Jenny. And there's still plenty of time," Nick pointed out. "He's in his middle forties, isn't he?"

"Right again." The conversation was no longer to Jenny's liking, but she tried to conceal her feelings. People invariably cross-examined her about her father's plans and she had learned to satisfy their curiosity instead of exploding.

"Do you think he'd run," Nick persisted, "assuming he felt he had the support?"

"Would you like it if he were elected?" Jenny parried.

"Yes. In general he's been positive toward agriculture and business. Now you answer my question," Nick demanded. "What would make him say yes?"

Annoyed by Nick Butler's one-track mind, Jenny sniffed airily, "I'm not privy to his innermost thoughts. I've obviously made a mistake. It's Emerson Ross's daughter who interests you, not plain Jennifer Ross."

"You forget, Jenny, I didn't know Emerson was your father until a few minutes ago," Nick stated. "But since he's such an objectionable topic, I'll avoid him from now on."

Jenny felt petulantly childish in the face of his implied criticism. An awkward silence of some five minutes ensued until, with a sigh, Nick asked Jenny to tell him about her job. She was anxious to grasp any proffered olive branch, and answered in detail. Soon the conversation progressed to a relaxed discussion of the merits and drawbacks of California living.

After dinner, Nick suggested that they go out to the pool for a swim. The temperature was still in the 90's and Jenny decided that there was no way she could get herself into trouble at a public pool. She readily agreed.

She walked into the pool area several minutes later, and the vision of Nick Butler in a close-fitting maroon bathing suit was enough to unglue her carefully fabricated composure. As she had guessed from dancing with him, no superfluous flesh marred his lean frame—just solid, hard muscle covered with an enticing smattering of dark hair. At the moment his bronzed body was dripping from the quick swim he had apparently taken.

Jenny already knew that she found him far too attractive for her own good. And the attraction wasn't only physical—she had enjoyed her dinner with Nick more than any similar evening she could recall. She was so eager to spend more time with him that she ignored her common sense, which told her that she was a fool to risk getting involved with someone so overbearing and deceitful.

Her experience in growing up under the thumb of a domineering father had made her shy away from forceful men. She had chosen to date tractable boys who behaved themselves when it came to sex and did precisely as they were told when it came to everything else. If they transgressed, they were unceremoniously dumped.

But Nick Butler was no college boy to be teasingly strung along. In many ways he reminded Jenny of her bulldozing father. She continued to stare but was not even aware that she *was* staring at him until her gaze reached his eyes—blue eyes that regarded her with mocking amusement.

A few long strides placed him beside her. "Well? What's the verdict? Yesterday you told me that I was an old man. Am I in good shape for my advanced age?"

"Yes," Jenny managed to mumble, "and also plenty conceited about it!"

He took her arm and firmly pulled her toward the water. "Come on, Jenny. You can appease that temper of yours by pushing me into the pool."

Jenny did so, laughing along with Nick as he did a comical sprawl off the side. Then he borrowed a rubber ball from some teenagers and initiated a diving, splashing game of catch. After fifteen minutes, breathless from the exercise and thoroughly outclassed, Jenny begged off. She collapsed into a lounge chair and watched Nick continue the game with the boys who had loaned him the ball.

It was quite dark out; the only illumination came from the artificial lighting surrounding the pool. Nick and his teenaged friends eventually abandoned their game because it was too difficult to spot the dark-colored ball in the dimly lit pool.

People began to leave and Nick walked over to the diving board to practice diving. Naturally, Jenny thought to herself, he would be very good at it. The quiet and darkness were soporific and she soon abandoned the attempt to keep awake. The last thing she remembered was a splash as Nick hit the water.

"Jenny!" The shout interrupted her light doze. "Come back in the water." Her eyes fluttered open to see Nick leaning against the side of the now-empty pool.

"I'm too sleepy for playing games," she objected with a yawn. "Go back to your diving."

Nick emerged from the pool and trotted over to her chair, the water from his body dripping onto her stomach. "Not," he said softly, "the kind of game I have in mind."

The next instant she found herself snatched up in his arms, being carried toward the pool and down the steps into the water. She began to wiggle and twist to gain her freedom. "Nick, someone could come," she hissed fiercely.

"They've all left; didn't you notice?" He tossed her, writhing all the while, out of his arms to arc ungracefully through the air and land with a considerable splash in the water. He laughed as she rose sputteringly to the surface.

Jenny stood no chance of escaping. Besides, she realized, she didn't want to escape. Nick wrapped his hands around her waist like a determined vine, then lifted her high out of the water until her stomach was level with his face. His mouth caressed her navel, then nibbled its way upward as he slowly lowered her into the pool. Her hands clung to his shoulders as his mouth teased her neck and face on this downward journey. She was pressed intimately against his body, the warm water around them adding to the shattering sensuality of Nick's playful lovemaking.

"How convenient that we're alone," he whispered against her lips. He slowly lowered her the rest of the way into the water, releasing her waist when her toes touched the bottom of the pool. One arm dropped down to slip underneath the elastic of her swimsuit, caressing her hip. The hardness of his body contrasted exquisitely with the silky feel of the wet hair on his chest and thighs.

It was agonizing torture for Jenny because Nick was so deliberate in his actions. She had raised her head for his kiss, twining one hand around his neck and holding his waist with the other. But he buried his face in her hair, nuzzling her shoulder, neck and face. By the time his mouth approached hers, she was shaking with arousal and anticipation, her head tipped back, eyes closed, lips softly parted in invitation.

His kiss was slow, thorough, and bruisingly passionate. Jenny returned it with fervent intensity, her usually staunch defenses totally destroyed. She was overwhelmed by what Nick was doing to her, not just with his mouth, which continued to dominate hers with deep, almost brutal kisses, but with his hands, which stroked her naked skin with devastating results.

Suddenly the sounds of talking and laughter reached her ears. Nick calmly released her, and Jenny was grateful that her back was to the intruders. Still trembling with arousal, she gazed up at him in confusion. His expression was bland, as though he was totally unaffected by what had just taken place between them. A group of teenagers was approaching the pool, their whistles and shouts of "Sorry folks" indicating that they were well aware of what they had interrupted.

Nick slipped an arm over Jenny's shoulder and nudged her gently toward the steps. "Time to go inside, I think. I'll walk you to your room."

As they emerged from the water, Jenny felt the interested eyes of four adolescent males on her body.

Nick smiled at them. "What are you guys doing back here? You couldn't have spent my thirty bucks already!"

"We got sick of playing your pinball machines, Mr. Butler," one of the boys said with a laugh. "You should put in a few other kinds."

"So where's my change?" Nick laughed. Jenny, held captive by the arm placed possessively around her shoulders, was doing a slow burn at the realization that he had actually paid the boys to disappear.

"We left it at the registration desk," another boy volunteered. "We figured you'd be done by now."

Nick began to walk toward the lounge chairs and their towels and robes, forcing a stiff-backed Jenny along with him. "Just for the record," he tossed back over his shoulder, "I'm walking the lady to her room, where she will go to sleep—alone." He draped a towel over Jenny's shoulders and led her from the pool area. In spite of Nick's gentlemanly disclaimer, she knew that the imaginative teenagers were picturing a vastly different end to the scene.

And it could easily have happened. Not out by the pool, perhaps, but Jenny knew that if Nick had picked her up and carried her to her room, her common sense wouldn't have stood a chance against the wanton cravings he so easily aroused in her.

When they reached the door to her room, Nick pulled out his key, presumably another master key, and unlocked the door. "There's no need to see me in," Jenny said tautly. "Why don't you go collect your change?"

He ignored her sarcasm, pulling her into the room and shutting the door behind them. He leaned against it, speaking in a soft, amused tone. "I don't apologize for paying them off. I wanted to be alone with you and I figured the pool was safer than your room. I do apologize for letting things get out of hand, Jenny. You're as passionate as you are hot-tempered, and I think I'd better leave before something else happens."

"You're not that irresistible," Jenny said haughtily. In her usual volatile manner, she was no longer annoyed with Nick for bribing the teenagers. Now she was annoyed at him because he wanted to walk out, without a word about getting in touch with her again.

He gave an impatient sigh and turned around. He was about to open the door when Jenny put out her hand to grip his right arm, preventing him from leaving. What was it about this man, she wondered, that made her forget all the lessons and resolutions of her twenty-one years just because he kissed her? Or even looked at her, she admitted ruefully. She flushed at the thought, staring at the floor to hide her blushes from Nick's all-too-knowing eyes. She knew it would be best if he did just as he had said he would, and left her before anything more happened, but she also knew, guiltily, that if he did she would be more hurt than she had ever been before. Suddenly, she couldn't bear the thought that she would never see him again.

"Yes?" Nick was still facing the door, and Jenny thought to herself that judging from his tone his face must be absolutely grim.

"Can't we talk?" she said uncertainly.

Nick turned, his eyes stabbing her with disapproval. "Is that what you want to do, talk?"

"No," she admitted in an aching whisper, and wound sinuous arms around his still-damp neck. She pressed a softly submissive mouth against his hard one.

Nick's subsequent shove was anything but gentle. A

startled Jenny staggered back, almost falling down in the process of trying to regain her balance. She was so humiliated by Nick's rejection that she turned her back to him, shaking, and waited for him to stalk out of the room. But she heard no aggressively slammed door, only a tensely snarled out declaration. "For Pete's sake, Jenny, your father is dead right when he says you need protecting. He never should have let you out of Davis! You can't hop into bed with a guy you've only known for thirty-six hours!"

All the men Jenny had met would have been delighted with a gentle kiss after triple that length of time, but Nick Butler was not to know that. "Hop into bed? Is that what you think I wanted?" she asked in a low, hurt voice as she turned to face him.

"That's exactly what I think," he said with impatient exasperation. "It's certainly not making love, that involves two people who care about each other. We're almost total strangers." He uttered a low curse, and when he continued, his voice was markedly more gentle. "Look, Jenny. It's obvious you're a virgin. A rather inexperienced virgin, in fact. I found your reactions amusing at first, but things have gone far enough. Now go to sleep. You've got a long drive ahead of you tomorrow."

Jenny summoned up the last vestiges of her pride and managed to inject an icy note into her voice. "I'm sorry my inexperience was so stultifying, Mr. Butler. But there *is* one saving grace. I'll reach Scottsdale tomorrow. No more motel rooms. Since I've ceased to amuse you, you must be delighted that you'll never have to see me again."

"Right," Nick said, and now he was smiling at her. "I'll never have to see you again. And do you still believe in Santa Claus, too?" With a shake of his head, he let himself out of the room.

Jenny was about to burst into tears, but Nick's last teasing comment left her thoroughly bemused. There was no doubt in her mind that he was telling her that they *would* see each other again. Perhaps he planned to look her up in Scottsdale.

But his comment could be taken another way, Jenny suddenly realized. He might mean that although he didn't particularly *want* to see her again, circumstances were such that he would *have* to. He had been unusually interested in Emerson Ross and his plans. *Had* he promised her father that he would keep an eye on her? And if he had, what would he be getting in return?

Chapter Three

The irrigated green fields outside of Coachella the next morning were the last lush cultivation Jenny passed for miles. The mountains in the distance were brown, bare of vegetation except for the occasional trees and low bushes that clung tenaciously to their slopes.

Nick Butler's truck was gone by the time Jenny emerged from her room at 7:30 that morning. She had stopped at a nearby restaurant for breakfast, ordering a large helping of bacon, eggs and hashbrowns. She would not make the mistake of trying to drive straight through to Scottsdale on an almost empty stomach.

She blushingly remembered her actions of the previous evening. She acknowledged that Nick Butler had a sabotaging effect on her previously reliable self-control. She had been overwhelmed by his sheer male virility and thoroughly captivated by his intelligence and charm. When he touched her, she found herself aching to do things she had always considered foolish or even immoral. It was humiliating to recall the occasions on which she had self-righteously scolded friends for becoming carried away, ridiculing their knowing protests that sooner or later the same thing would happen to her.

Now she admitted that the chemistry between herself and Nick had resulted in an explosion which she lacked the experience to handle. How could she have allowed herself to forget both his dishonesty and her own well-grounded suspicions? Her first priority upon arriving in Scottsdale would be to uncover the facts about the wealthy and arrogant Mr. Nicholas Joshua Butler, Jr., his myriad companies and his relationship with her father. She knew she had learned something from the humiliation and shame she had suffered when, after her unbridled and unappreciated passion of the previous evening, he had so coldly rejected her. Her cheeks burned when she thought about how wantonly she had thrown herself at Nick. It wouldn't happen again.

Surrounding Blythe, just short of the Arizona-California border, were more irrigated fields, but beyond them the country was barren, brown, empty. Jenny felt uneasy driving through it alone. From time to time cars and trucks whizzed by, heading west. Eastbound traffic was even lighter. Even though Jenny had checked the water level in the radiator when she stopped for gas that morning and found it to be full, she knew she would be thoroughly relieved once she entered the suburban fringes of Phoenix.

She was admiring several skyscraping specimens of saguaro cactus when she noticed smoke emerging from under her hood. Panic-stricken, she immediately stopped the car in the right-hand emergency lane and then simply sat inside, staring worriedly at the escaping puffs of white. With a sigh, she released the catch of the hood and got out of the car to examine the engine.

The intense heat which greeted her was no worse than that in Bakersfield or Indio. Unhappily, she was no longer lounging by a swimming pool but standing in the middle of a brutal desert. She checked the water level again; it was still full. But some other gadget among all that incomprehensible machinery was smoking, and Jenny could smell the burning electrical scent of it.

She had passed a number of highway patrol cars as she drove, but saw none now. Although several cars and trucks zoomed by, no one stopped to help her. She had been standing by the car some ten minutes when a glance across the freeway registered the approach of a large, familiar, silver-sided truck with black letters reading AMT on its side. But since it was headed west, toward Los Angeles, how could it possibly be Nick?

As the truck passed, an all too familiar driver greeted her with a friendly wave and a blast of his horn. Nick traveled several hundred yards further to a dirt turn-around and doubled back to stop a short distance behind Jenny's disabled car. After fifteen minutes in the sun, Jenny was sweating profusely from the relentless heat of this barren terrain, her t-shirt and shorts sticking to her body. She regarded the approach of the tall, amused-looking man with wary appreciation.

"So we meet again," he drawled at her, not the least bit abashed. "Having a problem with the car?"

Jenny was so taken aback by his casual attitude that she could only point soundlessly at the smoking engine.

Nick bent forward and carefully examined it. After a few moments Jenny gathered her scattered wits and stuttered, "How did you—I mean, you were coming from the wrong direction."

Nick looked up from the engine, his face bland. "I'm psychic. I was driving east and suddenly a picture flashed into my mind: Jennifer Ross, calling out to me for help. I turned around and came back."

Nick's silvery sunglasses prevented Jenny from reading the expression in his eyes, but his mouth had begun to crinkle up at the corners. Her temper began to simmer as she realized that he was amusing himself at her expense.

"I never called out to you for help," she snapped irritably. "You're about the last person I wanted to see when—"

"Fine," Nick interrupted. He turned and strode briskly back toward his truck. "See you around, Jenny."

She cursed her temper for the trouble it invariably landed her in and trotted after him, panting from the heat. As her hand tugged at his sleeve, she said breathlessly, "I'm sorry, Nick. Please don't leave."

He stopped. "You're finally learning." Taking her arm, he led her back to the car and pointed to something under the hood. "You've got a problem with the air-conditioning system," he explained evenly. "It's not a major repair, it would take about half an hour if they had the right part. So you have two choices. One, you can stop to get it fixed—there's an exit a few miles down the road. Or two, I can disconnect the system and you can go on to Scottsdale. You're not that far in terms of miles, but the highway isn't finished yet and it's going to take you a good hour and fifteen minutes to reach my . . . to get there." He folded his arms across his chest and waited for Jenny's decision.

She was too preoccupied by her predicament to wonder what he had been about to say before he changed his mind. She chewed on her lower lip and looked up at him, her expression uncertain. "Can I—is it safe to drive if you disconnect it?"

"Hot, but safe," Nick told her with a grin. "Don't worry, I'll follow you most of the way. I really do have to go down to Tucson today."

She might have objected to Nick's tailing her in the past, but not now. His offer decided the matter. "Then I—I'd rather not stop." She found herself dangerously close to tears, and could not understand why. She almost never cried. "I guess I'm lucky you came back," she admitted hoarsely, "but I still don't understand how you knew . . ."

"Another time, Jenny. Come on now, get a hold of yourself. You'll be more comfortable if you find something to wet down and wrap around your neck. I'll get you some water from the truck."

Jenny fished out her terry cloth cover-up from the suitcase and watched as Nick walked back from his truck, carrying a large plastic bottle. He soaked the robe with water and slung it around her neck, then performed some magical operation on her engine. Finally, he subjected her to a brisk, almost impersonal, little pat on her bottom before instructing her to start on her way.

Savoring the cool sensation of the terry cloth against her skin, Jenny resumed driving. The rest of the trip, through town after town and traffic light after traffic light, was hot but uneventful. She was relieved when the freeway resumed near Phoenix. She acknowledged Nick's toot with a grateful wave of her hand as she exited at Scottsdale while he continued on to Tucson.

She followed the directions she had been given and soon pulled up next to a booth housing a private guard, which served as a checkpoint for those who wished to enter the housing complex where the Hermanns lived. She introduced herself, saying that she was their new housekeeper; the man seemed to have been told to expect her since he directed her, without further questioning, to their home.

A high white stone wall enclosed the entire area, making it impossible to enter or exit except by going past the guard. Each house was different and all of them looked expensive. The most striking thing to Jenny's northern California eye was the absence of grass in the front yards. Desert landscaping prevailed. The front yards were pebbled, the gardens planted with different varieties of cactus, yucca and other desert plants. Jenny found the effect stark and arid-looking, but somehow very attractive.

By the time she staggered to the Hermanns' front door and rang the bell, an hour and a half without air conditioning had turned her into a wilted, bedraggled creature. She was embarrassed to meet her new employers in such a state, but told herself that it could hardly be helped.

The door was opened by a tall, slim, salt-and-pepper haired woman with striking blue eyes. She seemed stunned by Jenny's appearance, and hastily cut off the girl's halting introduction and apology. "My goodness, you look half dead. Come in here! And I'm Marian Hermann."

A very welcome blast of cold air soothed Jenny's

overheated body. "I had a problem with the car, Mrs. Hermann. I had no air conditioning for the last part of the trip."

"You sit down and I'll get you something cool to drink," Marian Hermann clucked. She led Jenny into the kitchen and poured her a glass of lemonade which her parched young employee drank down without pausing for breath. It was immediately refilled by the concerned Mrs. Hermann. This time Jenny sipped it with slow appreciation.

"Other than that, how was your trip?" Mrs. Hermann asked as she and Jenny sat down at the butcher block dinette table.

"It was—uneventful," Jenny lied. "I enjoyed some of the scenery though, especially the Joshua trees and the saguaro cactus."

"Good!" Mrs. Hermann smiled her approval. "Our desert vegatation takes some getting used to. As does our summer heat."

"It's not that much worse than where I come from," Jenny assured her. "At least, during our hot spells it's about like this. Is your granddaughter here, Mrs. Hermann?"

"Off swimming with my husband this afternoon. We thought we'd give you a few hours to unpack and relax. The things you shipped out from Davis arrived yesterday, by the way. I put them in your room."

Jenny's mother had given her a thorough lecture about asking her employer to specify her duties at the outset. She decided to broach the subject immediately. "What exactly—I mean, what hours will I work and what will my responsibilities be?"

Marian Hermann's eyes twinkled. "We expect breakfast in bed every morning and always eat our meals at three separate times. I want the house dusted and vacuumed twice a day, and my granddaughter is a hyperactive terror who needs constant attention if she isn't to wreck the house. In addition, Jenny, when Nicholas is in town, we'll send you over to his house to warm his bed. He eats sweet young things like you for breakfast!"

"Nicholas?" Jenny blurted out. She was quite content to go along with Mrs. Hermann's teasing until the mention of that name. But of course she meant Nicholas Hermann, Jenny thought with relief.

"My son. He'll be back in a few days. Have you had any lunch, dear?"

Jenny shook her head. "Not yet, Mrs. Hermann. I'd love something to eat, if you just show me where things are. And then I'd like to get the car fixed, if you could tell me where to go."

"I'll call the garage and tell them you'll be in. As for lunch, you run along and get cleaned up while I fix you a sandwich. Then you can see to your car."

Jenny followed her through a door off the kitchen; her bedroom and bath were beyond. It was a pleasant, if unpretentious, room, furnished with a lime green carpet, oak furniture, and an upholstered chair, drapes and bedspread in shades of cream and green. At the moment, the cartons containing Jenny's possessions were stacked on a dresser.

"Perhaps later you'll have time to lie down and sleep for a while. Although I must warn you that when Kitty comes back, she'll probably barge right in. Maybe you can teach her some manners, at times she's just like her father, never stopping for the niceties." Mrs. Hermann's indulgent tone told Jenny that she was not really serious.

A cool shower was at the top of Jenny's priority list and soon she was letting the refreshing water cascade down her back. Afterward, she pulled on fresh clothing, brushed her hair, and walked back to the kitchen.

A plate containing an egg salad sandwich, potato chips and carrot sticks was sitting on the table. "What would you like to drink?" Mrs. Hermann asked. "Milk? Iced tea? Lemonade? Soda?"

"You run some restaurant," Jenny laughed. "I'd love some more of your lemonade. I feel more like a guest than an employee."

"Don't worry about that." Mrs. Hermann poured another glass of lemonade and set it on the table. "You'll earn your salary, I promise you."

While Jenny ate, Mrs. Hermann gave her directions to a local service station which, luckily for Jenny, had a mechanic on duty even on a Saturday. His name was George and Mrs. Hermann assured Jenny that he was a mechanical wizard who would soon have her car running perfectly. The station was only a few miles away, but Jenny was sweltering by the time she pulled the car up to one of the service bays. A gray-haired man, his face deeply tanned and weathered by sun and age, approached her as she got out of the car. "You from the Hermanns?" he asked.

The embroidery on his shirt pocket identified him as the "George" she had been told to look for. "Yes, and Mrs. Hermann told me you can fix anything. Thank you for looking at my car." She unlatched the hood and watched apprehensively as he examined the engine.

"No problem. Needs a new belt. One or two other problems with the cooling system." He began to point to various pieces of equipment under the hood, explaining tersely what needed to be fixed. Jenny felt a rush of relief that he seemed to know what was wrong. "I'd really appreciate it if you could check the car out completely, George," she requested sweetly, her tone so irresistibly winsome that even the taciturn George succumbed to its charm. His leathery face broke out in a smile as he agreed to put the car up on the hoist and have a look underneath.

He directed Jenny to a small, air-conditioned office to wait, assuring her that if he found no further problems, the car would be ready in about an hour.

She had just exhausted the local reading matter when he strolled back into the office. "Car's finished," he announced. He held up a metal object, the shape of a hockey puck but smaller. "You with the CIA?" he asked.

Jenny stared at it, bewildered. "What do you— what's that? Is it part of my car?"

"Transmitter. Someone wants to tail you, he puts this on your car. Sends out a signal to the receiver in his car. Just like on television." Jenny rose from her seat and walked over to take the object in her hand. George watched her, one eyebrow cocked in inquiry.

Jenny felt her face heat up with anger. Now she knew how Nick had managed to keep such close tabs on her. Forcing herself not to raise her voice, she said stiffly, "It seems my father had me followed down here. He's very over-protective."

George only chuckled. "Can't say I blame him, Miss. If I had a daughter who looked like you, I'd keep a watch on her too."

They walked back over to the car, George handing Jenny a clipboard holding an itemized bill, which she paid in thoughtful silence. Back at the Hermanns, she exchanged a few polite sentences with her employer, thanking her for her help and asking permission to use the phone to call her parents to let them know she had arrived safely. The housekeeper, Emiko, answered; they chatted for several minutes before Jenny hung up and escaped to her room.

Only once she was alone did she allow her temper full rein. Nick Butler had followed her right from Davis, and she had never known because with the transmitter on her car he could stay considerably behind her—or ahead of her. And he had told her he was psychic! The sheer effrontery of it made her boil! She airily dismissed the relief she had felt when he appeared to rescue her.

Jenny detected the fine hand of Emerson Ross in all this, but it remained for her to find out precisely how and why. She was debating her future course of action when fatigue overcame anger. She fell into a heavy, exhausted sleep.

"Kitty, no! Wait!" As Marian Hermann had predicted, her granddaughter lost no time in making the acquaintance of her new baby sitter. The child opened the door and promptly bounced down onto Jenny's bed. Mrs. Hermann's apologetic look was smilingly acknowledged by Jenny, who assured her that she was as anxious to meet Kitty as Kitty was to meet her.

The young girl greeted her with an effusive, "Hi! I'm Nichole. But everybody calls me Kitty. Daddy named me Kitty because I had fuzzy fur on my head when I was a baby and everyone still calls me that."

Jenny smiled sleepily at Kitty's adult tone as she related this tale. "Hi Kitty. I'm Jenny. Did you enjoy your swim?"

Kitty's head bobbed up and down enthusiastically.

"Yes. I know freestyle and breast stroke and back-stroke and I just learned the butterfly. Next year I'm going to swim on a swim team like I did in California."

Whatever else the child was, Jenny told herself, she certainly wasn't shy or averse to being questioned. Jenny asked curiously, "Where do you swim?"

"At Daddy's. We have a pool there. Do you like to swim? Because if you do, you could take me there tomorrow. I don't need a lifeguard, but Daddy won't let me swim alone."

Jenny was amused by Kitty's pleading face. "He's right, too. And I'd love to go there tomorrow." She searched for some innocuous subject with which to continue the conversation, coming up with, "Were you named after your father?"

"Sort of," Kitty chirped. "Daddy is actually Nicholas, Jr. I was supposed to be a boy, I would have been Nicholas the third." She giggled. "Nicholas isn't a very good name for a *girl,* is it? So I'm Nichole."

Jenny felt like she had walked into a mystery play at the end of the first act. "I thought your grandfather's name was Oscar. Is that his middle name?"

"Oscar?" Kitty asked in a puzzled voice. Then her head bobbed up and down. "Oh! You mean *that* grandpa! He's just like a real grandpa but he's not Nicholas Sr. That was Daddy's father. He's dead."

"You mean Grandpa Oscar is actually your grandmother's—second husband?" An uncomfortable weight had settled itself high in Jenny's stomach but she was determined to ignore the suspicions that were crowding her mind.

"Uh-huh. Grandpa Oscar and Grandma got married before I was born. He has a daughter in New York—I call her Aunt Mary—and I have three cousins that are almost grown up. I've only met them a few times." The child's expression turned wistful. "When I was four, I moved to California with my mother. Daddy used to visit a lot, but I only got to see Grandma and Grandpa when I came to Scottsdale. Mommy wouldn't let them visit."

The conversation had taken too serious a turn for Jenny's peace of mind. It was clear to her that Kitty had experienced some traumatic events in her nine years and she wished fervently that there had been time to learn some of the family's history from her employer. She said lightly, "But you're living here now, so you can see them all the time."

She had no sooner uttered the words when she realized her mistake. Kitty's voice was eerily matter-of-fact as she said, "Sure. Mommy's dead." Jenny was no child psychologist, but she remembered reading that it was best not to be evasive or secretive with children. So she merely asked, "Do you want to tell me anything about it?"

"She drowned," Kitty replied tonelessly. Her dark head drooped against her chest, her long hair concealing her expression.

Jenny had no idea what to say. She was afraid of making another terrible blunder. Fortunately, Kitty seemed to recover quickly, telling Jenny, "I look just like Daddy." She began to play with her hair, braiding the dark strands. "Are you going to be here a long time?"

Something in the child's tone told Jenny that she was seeking reassurance; she wanted to know if she could trust Jenny. "I hope so, Kitty. It's a good place for me to sell the jewelry I make and I think Scottsdale is a beautiful town. Your grandma is a very nice lady and I think you and I could be good friends. I have no reason to want to leave."

Kitty nodded solemnly. "If I ask you something, you promise not to tell I asked?"

Heaven only knows what's coming now! Jenny thought in dismay. But she gave her promise.

"Well, if I look like Daddy, does that prove I'm his daughter?" The child continued to pull nervously at her hair.

"Of course you're his daughter." Jenny said as soothingly as she could. She tried to hide her horror at the question, wondering just what sort of family she had come to work for. "One look at you and your grandmother and anyone could tell you're related."

The answer seemed to satisfy Kitty. As for Jenny, she had only one additional question—a question to which she already knew the answer. "Kitty, what's your full name?"

"Nichole Jennifer Butler. Jennifer, just like you. So I have the same initials as Daddy, because he's Nicholas Joshua, Jr." She yawned. "I have to go take a nap now, otherwise Grandma won't let me stay up to watch T.V. Will you wake me if I sleep too long?"

Jenny, her emotions seesawing between shock and fury, promised to do so. Her young charge obediently skipped off to her bedroom for the ordered rest.

Alone, Jenny conjured up a mental picture of Nick Butler. How could she have failed to notice the resemblance between Kitty and her father? It was so obvious that it should have struck her the moment Kitty opened the door. Given that fact, it made no sense that Nick should have doubts about his paternity—doubts which had been conveyed to his daughter. It must have been some marriage! she thought to herself. Her heart went out to Kitty, and she wondered how long it had been since the child's mother had died.

. Sympathy for Kitty soon gave way to other, less charitable emotions, however. The flash of irritation Jenny felt with her father was minor compared to her steaming resentment toward Nick. The man had played with her like a sleek, healthy tomcat does when he catches a hapless mouse. Jenny almost hated him for it.

As for her father, he had dropped his stringent objections to her leaving home with suspicious suddenness, and obviously Nick Butler was the reason. The two of them must have engaged in some old-fashioned political horse trading. Had her father asked Nick to follow her down to Scottsdale? Or had Nick offered to do so?

There was no time like the present to learn the answer. Jenny brushed her hair, straightened her clothing and marched into the living room. Just short of the doorway, she slowed her step to a casual gait. Dr. and Mrs. Hermann were sitting on a flower-printed couch, sipping cold drinks. She shook hands upon being introduced to Dr. Hermann, complimenting her employers on the charm of the room. The plush, sand-colored carpet blended beautifully with the subdued burnt orange and browns of the couch, which were repeated in the comfortable looking armchairs grouped nearby. Paintings by western and Indian artists were arranged on the walls. A baby grand piano sat in one corner of the room, and Jenny's eye was caught by the photographs resting on top of it.

"Are those pictures of your family?" Her tone held no more than polite interest.

Marian Hermann rose, motioning Jenny over to the piano. "This is Nicholas and Kitty at Disneyland, with Mickey Mouse," Mrs. Hermann explained, lightly touching the framed picture. "And this is Oscar's daughter and her family, on a ski trip to Quebec. And our wedding picture, Oscar and I will be celebrating our tenth anniversary in another few weeks. My son was the matchmaker."

She took Jenny's arm and led her to a wall unit containing books, stereo equipment and a wonderful collection of intricately woven, colorful baskets. "My first husband," she said, indicating a picture of a man posed next to an airplane, "and Oscar's first wife. And now you've seen all of us."

She certainly had, especially Nick, who had been caught looking at Kitty with a mixture of sadness and love. She knew that she would never see such an expression on his face when he looked at her.

They sat down on the couch, and Jenny accepted a glass of white wine from Dr. Hermann. "Well, I've met Kitty and I think she's adorable, although I may have trouble keeping up with her," Jenny said with a smile. "I'm sure I'll enjoy working down here." She paused and contrived a slight frown. "But you know, I'm surprised my father let me come. I had the worst time convincing him, and I was amazed when he changed his mind." She smiled at Oscar Hermann. "You must be a miracle worker."

"I did speak to your father," Dr. Hermann explained in his gruff but pleasant voice, which was tinged with a definite German accent. "He insisted you must finish college, and as a professor I sympathized with his viewpoint. But my cousin was so enthusiastic about you, and so supportive of your reasons for wishing to leave school, that I persisted." He gave a little chuckle. "I even called in the reinforcements."

"Reinforcements?" Jenny echoed, feigning confusion.

"My stepson. His company has business interests in California—agriculture, motels, recreation, trucking. There are times when Nicholas prefers to do his own lobbying. Recently the legislature has been considering a bill that imposes additional regulations on the trucking industry. Naturally, Nicholas is opposed to it; he has discussed the matter with your father more than once."

"Over the past few years, he's gotten to know your father quite well, Jenny," Mrs. Hermann chimed in. "Even though he chooses to make his home in Scottsdale, what happens in California is important to our business interests. Your father is a very fine assemblyman." She laughed softly. "The size of my son's donations to his campaigns stems as much from admiration as it does from politics!"

"So you told my father you were Nick—Nicholas's mother and stepfather?" The revelations thus far had surpassed anything Jenny expected to hear, and she wondered what else could possibly come out.

Dr. Hermann shook his head. "Actually, not at all. We were sharing lunch when Marian told Nicholas of the problems we were experiencing. He walked to the telephone, called your father's office, and arranged for you to come to us."

"My goodness," Jenny put in ingenuously, "what on earth did he do to make Daddy change his mind? Promise him a big contribution next time he runs?"

Marian Hermann looked shocked. "Jenny! Of course

he didn't. Nicholas simply told Emerson that he would appreciate it if he let you come to Scottsdale, as a personal favor."

"And promised to keep an eye on you, my dear," Dr. Hermann added, laughing robustly at the thought of it. "Hardly a disagreeable chore, to be sure. Ah well, I'm certain your father knew he was entrusting you to a worthy second family. What is closer to the heart of a politician than a major contributor?"

Marian Hermann regarded her husband with disapproval, which put no dent in his puckish good humor. "Tell me, Jenny, will your father run for governor?"

Not that again! Jenny thought to herself. But she answered with as much civility as she could muster. "I really don't know, Dr. Hermann. That ambition seems to be a graveyard for former speakers." Then, unable to help herself, she added acidly, "Even the persuasive powers of your stepson, great as they apparently are, might prove insufficient to convince him to take the risk."

The look exchanged by the Hermanns did not go unnoticed by Jenny. She felt like biting her tongue. But Oscar seemed to find her pique amusing. "Who is your fit of temper for, my dear?" he asked, his eyes lit with delight. "Your father or my stepson? Or both of them, for, shall we say, negotiating the terms under which you would be permitted to come here?"

The thought of it was altogether too much for Jenny's hot temper. "Terms? What terms?" she snapped.

"My goodness, Jenny, Oscar was only teasing you. I'm certain there was nothing more to it than a favor from your father to Nicholas," Mrs. Hermann interjected quickly. "I can see it's a subject best avoided. Tell us about the jewelry you make, dear."

Jenny was afraid she had offended her employers by speaking too sharply, and was relieved to change the subject. As she talked, Kitty appeared in the living room, her eyes still heavy with sleep, and curled up next to her grandmother on the couch. The Hermanns' attention shifted to their granddaughter, which gave Jenny the opportunity to digest what she had learned in the last half hour.

So Nicholas Joshua Butler, Jr. was not only an acquaintance of her father, she silently fumed, he was a major contributor, frequent lobbyist and ardent admirer. Her father's support could be vitally important to his business interests.

It explained so much about Nick's attitude toward her. Jenny had once thought to herself that he hardly seemed the honorable type. Much more likely, he would take what pleasures women offered him, leaving them brokenhearted the moment he became bored. But never with Emerson Ross's daughter. It was a splendid opportunity for him and Jenny had played right into his hands. She could picture the whole campaign, which would culminate with the two of them marching down the aisle of a church. As Emerson Ross's son-in-law, Nick's position would be the envy of every businessman in California. On the other hand, if Nick had been the man who seduced and abandoned her, Emerson would have him thrown out of his office the next time he showed up! Little wonder he had been careful to keep the lovemaking relatively innocent! The man was nothing but an opportunistic skunk!

Chapter Four

"Do you know how to use a food processor?"

Mrs. Hermann had motioned Jenny into the kitchen to help with dinner and now pointed to a counter containing every appliance known to woman.

Jenny nodded. "My mother has one." She busied herself feeding vegetables into the machine while her employer sliced up a marinated piece of steak. As they worked, Jenny again raised the subject of her duties. This time Mrs. Hermann's answer was a serious one.

"Once Kitty is in school, you'll have a great deal of free time. So I hope you won't mind working extra hours for the rest of the summer. I'd like you to plan on taking care of Kitty during the day. Most weekends she'll be with Nicholas. You'll be responsible for cleaning the house thoroughly once a week and also for the grocery shopping. We can cook dinner together."

Mrs. Hermann paused for several seconds,

prompting Jenny to glance up. She was about to murmur her acquiescence to Mrs. Hermann's instructions when the older woman continued thoughtfully, "Tell me, Jenny, are you a good cook?"

"Yes, especially Japanese food. Our housekeeper taught me, and she's Japanese," Jenny volunteered, puzzled by the question. "Will you want me to do some of the meals on my own?"

"Perhaps, but that's not why I asked. The fact is, Nicholas is a dreadful cook. He barbecues steaks and not much more. Would you mind terribly if I asked you to fix dinner for him and Kitty on the nights he's home?" Taking in Jenny's quick frown, she hurriedly added, "Of course, you wouldn't have to work for me on those evenings." Her forehead wrinkled in distress. "He refuses to come here for dinner more than once a week, and the result is that Kitty eats in restaurants far too often. If you wouldn't mind shopping and cooking for him, I'd be very grateful. At least I'd know that Kitty was being properly looked after."

There was no logical reason for Jenny to refuse since her hours would not be affected by Mrs. Hermann's request. But prancing around Nick Butler's kitchen was one of the last things she wanted to do; thinking of ways to avoid him had become one of her main concerns. Besides, the man was thirty-three years old, surely capable of taking adequate care of his own daughter. "I'd be in the way," she equivocated. "Your son wouldn't want a stranger intruding on his privacy."

"It would be a godsend," Mrs. Hermann coaxed. "Nicholas works very hard. When he comes home, he's tired, too tired to prepare decent meals, even if he knew how." She delivered the *coup de grace*. "Just ask poor little Kitty. She's already so tired of restaurants. She even told me how nice it would be once you came and could cook for her and her father."

In the face of such outrageous blackmail, Jenny felt she had no choice but to gracefully accede to Mrs. Hermann's wishes. She realized that Nick and his mother had more than a little in common: both of them were adept at getting their own way!

"All right, Mrs. Hermann, if it will make Kitty happy, I'd be pleased to cook for her and—and your son," Jenny agreed, trying to sound cheerful about the prospect. Hoping that the answer would be no, she went on, "Will there be anything else? Cleaning, or baby-sitting?"

"Heavens, no. He has a darling woman who comes in twice a week to clean. As for baby-sitting in the evenings, you can discuss it with Nicholas when he comes back from Tucson." Mrs. Hermann began to gather up the vegetables Jenny had sliced, carrying them over to the wok to stir-fry.

"When will he be back?" Jenny was grateful for the opportunity to insert the question into the conversation. She had been wondering about it ever since she discovered that Nick Butler was Kitty's father.

"Friday, I think. It depends how things go. But I do expect him for the weekend." Mrs. Hermann left the topic and proceeded to name a very generous monthly salary, asking if Jenny had any further questions.

Jenny had a whole list of questions, but none of them concerned her job. During dinner, she did manage to learn that Kitty had come to Scottsdale about four weeks before, and that Marcia Butler had died two months ago. She also found out that Dr. Hermann taught foreign literature at Arizona State University in nearby Tempe. Mrs. Hermann put in several days a week at the downtown office housing the headquarters of AMT, Inc., the company founded by her late husband and expanded by her son. The initials stood for Arizona Mining and Trucking, although the name had long ago become obsolete as the company acquired other interests, but Nick had preferred not to change it.

Now Jenny understood why the Hermanns needed help in caring for Kitty. With Dr. Hermann home for the summer break, they had managed to juggle their schedules to accommodate Nick's work and travel commitments but it had been difficult for them and would become more so once the university term began. It was obvious that both of them were very relieved that Jenny had finally arrived, and were content to give her a free hand in caring for Kitty. After twenty-one years of being dominated by Emerson Ross, such freedom and trust were sweet indeed.

Kitty, fully dressed, her long dark hair gathered into two ponytails and tied with yellow yarn, shook Jenny awake the next morning. "Guess what, Jenny?" The child's face was lit up with anticipation.

"What?" Jenny resisted the urge to brush Kitty's overlong bangs out of her eyes.

"I'm going to be ten on September 18th. And I already know what present I'm going to get from Daddy. An airplane ride over the Grand Canyon. I was thinking—you're going to be part of the family now, so you should come too. Okay?"

Kitty's tone was such that Jenny knew the child assumed she was offering some cherished opportunity.

As much as Jenny enjoyed sight-seeing, she promised herself she would avoid any treks throughout the southwest in the company of Nicholas J. Butler, Jr. She sensed that it was not the proper moment to make her position known to Kitty, however, and merely thanked her warmly and shooed her out of the room with a firmness that fooled no one, least of all Kitty.

As she showered, she did some quick mental arithmetic. Nick had told her that he was thirty-three; his daughter was almost ten. That meant Nick had married Kitty's mother when he was twenty-two or even younger. He made no pretense of having loved or even liked his late wife, and Jenny wondered just why he had married her. Nick had called Marcia Butler a tramp; had other men ruined their relationship?

Jenny dressed in shorts and a sleeveless top and opened the door to the kitchen to find that Mrs. Hermann had just finished making her an omelet for breakfast. She smiled her thanks, adding, "You're going to spoil me. I thought I was supposed to be cooking for you!"

Dr. Hermann soon joined them, and after a pleasant breakfast Jenny excused herself and went to find Kitty, who was in her room.

Jenny's eye was immediately caught by a photograph on the child's night table. It was a close-up of Kitty and a fair-haired, blue-eyed woman. No doubt she had once been lovely, but the camera revealed wrinkles about her eyes and mouth and a face that smiled with a certain brittle weariness. The woman appeared to be in her late thirties or even early forties, and Jenny wondered if she could possibly be Kitty's mother. She seemed too old, too hard.

The child soon put an end to her silent speculation. "She was beautiful, don't you think?" Kitty asked wistfully. "I miss her so much, especially when Daddy's away."

Jenny nodded. "Of course you do. It's only natural to miss her and remember her with love, Kitty. When was the picture taken?"

"A few months ago. Paul took it, he was Mommy's friend who lived with us."

Jenny was appalled, not only by this revelation but by the child's matter-of-fact tone. Kitty knew more of life at ten than Jenny had known at sixteen. If there had been some subtle way of discovering whether Nick and his wife had been divorced or merely separated, she would have done so. Instead, she simply nodded again, and suggested to Kitty that they spend the morning taking a drive around the area so that Jenny could learn her way around the city.

After 2½ hours of reconnoitering, including an early lunch at a hamburger stand and a side trip out to Taliesin West, once the home of architect Frank Lloyd Wright, Jenny and Kitty returned home. The Hermanns were gone, and had left a note saying they would be back late that afternoon.

"I know how to get to Daddy's house, Jenny. Let's go swimming. Please? It's not far and I'm so hot!" Jenny heartily concurred with Kitty's request. She gathered up suits and towels as Kitty wandered into the den, only to return and state with exasperation, "I can't find where Grandma put the keys."

Jenny supposed the girl meant the house keys. Even if the thought of exploring Nick's domain in his absence did have a certain seductive appeal, she knew there was no real excuse for entering the house. "We won't need the key; there's no need to go inside."

"Not for the house; for the gate," Kitty replied with the crushing tone that nine year olds reserve for dim-witted adults.

Although most homes in northern California were fenced, Jenny had not noticed that to be true in Scottsdale. "What gate is that?" she asked Kitty.

"The gate across the driveway. And we have to turn off the alarm system, otherwise when we unlock the gate, the alarm will go off."

Kitty made the house sound like a fortress. "Does your father get burglarized often?" Jenny asked incredulously.

Kitty shrugged. "I dunno. Nobody's robbed him since *I* came, so I guess it works." Jenny followed her back to the den and watched as she rummaged through her grandmother's desk, ultimately locating the keys in a metal file box. "I'll leave a note for Grandma and Grandpa to let them know we're at Daddy's," she announced. Jenny felt like she was the child and Kitty the baby-sitter.

Nick lived less than ten minutes from his mother and to Jenny's considerable amusement, she found it entirely appropriate that such an egotistical man had chosen to buy a home halfway up a mountain. Mount Camelback indeed resembled a camel, Jenny could pick out the head, ears and humped body. The road to Nick's house twisted up its side, the stucco and stone homes along the route custom-built and luxurious. Jenny had read that the area was nicknamed the "millionaires' ghetto."

Some of the houses had swimming pools and tennis courts; occasional signs along the way proclaimed "No

Trespassing—Private Driveway." As they approached one such daunting sign, Kitty told her to turn in. "Pull up and I'll unlock the gate, Jenny."

As the car idled, Kitty hopped out, turned a key in what must have been the alarm box and opened a large padlock. She pulled a length of chain away from the gate, which connected to a formidable steel fence which circled the property. After Jenny passed through, Kitty nonchalantly reversed the process and got back into the car.

After about fifty feet, Nick's home came into view. It was built into the hillside so that the back half was several feet higher than the front half. The drive ran parallel to the house for a dozen yards, then circled around to rejoin the route they had just taken.

In accordance with Kitty's instructions, Jenny left the car near the double garage at the right side of the house. A flagstone path led around the garage to the back.

Jenny thought to herself that the backyard looked like the domain of some Hollywood magnate. A separate building housed three cabanas, a bathroom and a large bar. The kidney-shaped pool was surrounded by a flagstone patio, on which were scattered lounge chairs and other deck furniture. Beyond the pool was a velvety, emerald lawn, still soaked by water from the sprinkler system necessary to keep the grass alive in this desert climate. A desert garden, highlighted by a trio of magnificent saguaro cacti, ringed the entire backyard.

The dining room, living room and, apparently, the master bedroom backed onto the patio. Although the windows of these rooms were covered by shutters or woven wood blinds to keep out the sun, Jenny could see part of the interior through a series of sliding glass doors. One end of the dining room table was visible, as were a softly shining parquet floor and part of a Navajo rug in the living room. Jenny could also make out the back of an off-white sofa. The bedroom door was shielded by draperies, and she caught a glimpse only of lush carpeting and a large mirror. She had to repress the urge to press her nose against the glass for a more thorough inspection.

Kitty was impatiently tugging her bikini from Jenny's arms. The child did not bother going into one of the cabanas to change, but stripped off her clothing right where she stood and tossed it on a circular, umbrella-shaded table.

The next moment she had wiggled into her suit and was removing the automatic pool sweeper which moved lazily through the water. Jenny glanced around her at the high foliage which screened the property, then decided that given their isolation there was no need to go into one of the cabanas to change and quickly followed Kitty's example.

She gave a strangled yelp as Kitty raced to the diving board and did a backward flip off the end. The child swam quickly to the shallow end of the pool, made an underwater turn worthy of an Olympic competitor, and swam back to the deep end. Jenny was more deliberate. She sat at the edge of the pool and dangled her feet in the water, then slid in.

After ten minutes of exercise, she emerged from the pool to sprawl out contentedly on a lounge chair. An impish Kitty followed her. "Want something to drink?" she asked with a grin.

"What's so funny?" Jenny demanded, struggling into a sitting position.

"*You* should pay *Daddy*," Kitty teased. "But I won't tell him how easy you have it. Gosh, I'm starved."

She darted off to the pool building. Kitty's comment made Jenny realize how relieved she was that the Hermanns were paying her salary. It would be galling to accept Nick Butler's money, not to mention his authority. But of course, the child could have no notion of the financial arrangements.

By the time Jenny reached the bar, Kitty had already prepared a tray of cheese and crackers. Jenny sat on a stool and nodded as Kitty held up a cola. Behind the bar were a double refrigerator, cabinets and a dazzling array of bottles. The room also contained a color television set and a number of cushioned chairs and love seats.

They ate their snack at the counter of the bar, taking the soft drinks outside to finish. Kitty spent most of the afternoon in the pool, diving, swimming and paddling around on a plastic inflatable raft. Jenny sunbathed, read and took an occasional dip in the water.

The hedonism of the afternoon was interrupted by the demanding sound of a ringing telephone. Kitty dashed out of the water to the pool house to answer it, returning several minutes later with a huge grin plastered on her face. "It's for you," she announced.

Wondering what was so amusing, Jenny went into the bar and picked up the phone. "Mrs. Hermann?" she asked uncertainly. "Did you want us to come home?"

"Try again," the male voice on the other end of the line ordered drily. "Having a tough afternoon?"

Jenny's whole body stiffened with resentment. She had learned enough about Nick Butler's duplicity to ache to tear him limb from limb, but there was no way to do that over the phone. So she simply answered icily, "Very. Was there anything else, *Mr.* Butler?"

"Ahh," he drawled, "you're annoyed with me." There was a pause, as if he were waiting for Jenny to lose her temper. She bit back the angry tirade that hovered on her lips, determined to wait until she had the dubious pleasure of delivering it in person.

Nick laughed softly. "I called my mother's, got no answer, and thought I'd try the house. I wanted to see if Kitty liked you as much as I thought she would. And she does. I'll try to get home Wednesday or Thursday."

Again Nick paused for Jenny's reply, and again Jenny forced herself to remain silent instead of spitting out, "Don't hurry on my account." She angrily denied to herself that his silky voice was having any effect on her, other than to make her angry.

"Jenny? Are you still there?"

"Yes." The word was snapped out between clenched teeth.

"Right." Suddenly Nick's tone was businesslike. "Tell Mom I called. Tell her I need Sam with me. He's not at home so she'll have to track him down, he may be at our casino in Vegas. I'm at our motor inn near the airport. Have him call me as soon as possible."

"Oh, yes *sir*," Jenny said resentfully, wishing that Nick could see the accompanying sarcastic salute.

"Perhaps you'd better put Kitty back on," he said

with a sigh. "At least if I give her the message, I'll know that—"

"That won't be necessary," Jenny interrupted coldly. "I'll tell your mother what you said. And I'm sure that when this Sam of yours finds out that he's wanted by the great Nicholas J. Butler, Jr., he'll charter the next plane to Tucson!"

"He'd better," Nick laughed. "It's what I pay him for." He hung up the phone without saying good-bye.

Jenny repressed the urge to slam the receiver down. Damn the man for catching her off guard again! She had plenty of time between now and Thursday to think up an acid tongue-lashing for Nick Butler, and she intended to compose a tirade so blistering that it would make the 110° heat seem like an arctic storm!

Since it was close to five o'clock, Jenny decided that she and Kitty should be getting home. When they arrived at the Hermanns, Oscar and Marian were sitting at the kitchen table drinking iced tea. Kitty dropped onto her grandfather's lap for a hug and kiss as Jenny was passing on Nick's message to his mother.

"Sam Jacobson is our attorney," Mrs. Hermann remarked. "Nicholas is in Tucson to discuss the acquisition of a small mining company. Things must be moving rather quickly if he needs Sam down there tomorrow."

She disappeared into the den to try to locate the attorney. Twenty minutes later, she reemerged with a satisfied look on her face, announcing that Sam Jacobson had been located and would catch the next plane to Tucson. Jenny reflected grimly on the alacrity with which everyone jumped to do Nick's bidding. But she didn't happen to work for Nicholas J. Butler, and there

was no way in the world that she intended to take
orders from him!

During the next few days, Jenny spent the mornings
shopping and cleaning and the afternoons swimming
with Kitty. On Monday, Kitty had confided that she
loved to swim without a suit. Jenny had noticed the
child's all over tan the previous afternoon and since the
pool was completely private she had no objections. She
refused Kitty's coaxing suggestion that she do the same,
however, but compromised to the extent of floating
around the pool on the inflated raft, lying on her
stomach, with her top off in order to prevent a strap
mark across her back.

Jenny was pleased at how quickly Kitty's attachment
to her had developed. Hugs and kisses seemed entirely
natural, and the two often walked arm in arm while
running errands. Like most girls her age, Kitty was
bubblingly loquacious. She spoke easily and frequently
of her father and mother, often mentioning her mother's men friends but never her father's other women.
Since Jenny knew from personal experience that Nick
was a normal human male, she assumed that he made it
a practice to shield Kitty from a knowledge of his social
life.

Every now and then Kitty made some comment
which reminded Jenny that the child had endured some
traumatic events in her young life. On one occasion,
Jenny had complimented her on her swimming, and
Kitty had replied sadly, "Mommy wanted me to learn
because she never really did. Maybe if she had . . ."
Her voice trailed off and Jenny had changed the
subject. She was aware that Marcia Butler had

drowned and it seemed that Kitty felt guilty for not being able to save her. Had the child actually been present at the time?

On another occasion, Kitty was telling Jenny about a trip she had taken to Mexico with her mother and a man named Stephen. Since the vacation had taken place only the previous Christmas, Jenny had asked without thinking, "Don't you mean Paul?"

The answer had been almost petulant. "Stephen. He was the one before Paul." Kitty had continued with a description of Acapulco, but Jenny listened with only half an ear. She wondered with horror if the woman changed boyfriends as often as she changed the oil in her car. For a few moments she actually felt sorry for Nick Butler, but then she told herself that if the man had been the same arrogant, unrepentant liar at twenty-three as he was at thirty-three, it was little wonder that his wife behaved badly.

Nick called again on Tuesday, speaking briefly to his mother and for several more minutes to Kitty. Jenny and Mrs. Hermann were preparing dinner as Oscar sat and chatted with them, and judging from Kitty's end of the conversation, Nick Butler was questioning the girl about what she and Jenny had been doing with themselves for the past two days.

At one point Kitty giggled, "Yup. But Jenny won't. I think she's afraid someone will come." Jenny was certain that her face had turned scarlet, and a surreptitious glance at Oscar Hermann's twitching mouth embarrassed her still further when she realized that the older man was obviously aware of the subject under discussion.

Mrs. Hermann took the phone back from her granddaughter, concluding with, "I will dear. We'll see you tomorrow night, then, for dinner. Bye now."

Then she turned to Jenny. "He says to tell you he's looking forward to meeting you." And if Marian Hermann wondered why Jenny's smile appeared so forced when she murmured, "Me too," she made no mention of it.

Chapter Five

By Wednesday afternoon, an unsettling edginess had overtaken Jenny. Nick had told his mother that he would try to be home for dinner; Jenny was certain that the meal would prove to be an ordeal. To pretend that she had never met Nick Butler when she longed to pour a drink over his head would exceed both her abilities as an actress and her lamentably lacking control over her temper.

She and Kitty went to the pool that afternoon, as usual, but she couldn't enjoy herself as she normally did. She tried to work off her nervousness with activity, challenging Kitty to race her for several laps, and when she finished she was exhausted—but far from calm.

After a while, Kitty announced that she was going into the house to change and lie down, and suggested that Jenny come along and nap on Nick's waterbed. Jenny had no intention of doing any such thing. "I'm going to perfect my tan," she said with a weak smile. "If I get sleepy, I'll just doze on the raft."

With a shake of her head, as if to indicate that her baby-sitter was obviously crazy, Kitty went inside.

Jenny dove into the water and for several minutes floated on her back, staring up at the light blue, cloudless sky. Then she grabbed the plastic raft from the side of the pool, rolled onto it, and lay face down, her head buried in her left arm, her hair pulled off to one side to drift in the water. Her right arm made lazy lines in the water, propelling the raft aimlessly around the pool. After a while she reached back and untied her suit top, tossing the wisp of cotton to hang whimsically from the diving board. Without Kitty splashing and chattering the pool area was silent, and Jenny soon relaxed into a half sleep.

Some corner of her mind registered the rolling sound of a sliding glass door opening and then closing. The next sounds she heard were several vigorous thumps on the diving board, followed by a substantial splash. Her brain had just assimilated the fact that the sounds were far too loud to be caused by the sixty pound Kitty when she felt water being drizzled onto her back. Her head jerked up, her eyes encountering a curtain of heavy, damp hair. She raised a hand to impatiently push it aside and looked at the water in front of her. She saw no one. A glance at the diving board showed that her bikini top had been removed.

She couldn't slide off the raft—not without revealing far too much—so she craned her neck to glance back over her shoulder. Suddenly two strong, suntanned hands came up from underneath her to clamp themselves around the raft and her body. Jenny jerked her head back around, about to scream—and came face to face with a grinning Nick Butler.

It was not how she had envisioned their first moments alone together. She had had vague plans of luring him off to some secluded back road, where she would deliver the scalding setdown he deserved. Instead, the man had surprised her yet again, and she could only stammer, "What—what are *you* doing here?"

Nick released her to backstroke lazily away. He pulled himself out of the water and sat on the edge of the pool, droplets streaking down his sleek body. "I own this place, remember?" he drawled.

"As if I could forget," Jenny muttered under her breath. Her face flaming with embarrassment at Nick's wicked stare, she glanced around the perimeter of the pool to locate her bikini top. She could hardly castigate the high-and-mighty Nick Butler while lying face down on a plastic raft. Jenny soon spotted it on the side of the pool opposite where Nick sat and began to paddle over to it. Moments later there was a splash as Nick arched gracefully over Jenny's back, easily reaching the opposite side ahead of her.

"You set yourself up for this one," he laughed, dangling the top in front of her. Jenny glared at him impotently. "Why so shy? I'll bet you would have let me take it off a few nights ago," he teased.

Jenny was so incensed that her embarrassment was eclipsed by fury, especially because she knew he was right. "A few nights ago I didn't know that you were a lying— conniving—manipulative— deceitful— beast!" She emphasized each insulting word, then concluded, "As well as having the mentality of a thirteen year old!"

Nick slid into the water directly ahead of her. "You're right," he said with mock repentance, handing her the bikini top.

Jenny snatched it away from him. It was obvious that Nick Butler, far from being contrite, found the whole incident hugely amusing. This fact only served to make Jenny even more livid than she had been in the first place. "Turn around," she said waspishly.

"No way," Nick said with a lazy grin. "In deference to your wounded sensibilities, I'm keeping my hands off. Don't expect me to keep my eyes off also."

"You're obnoxious," Jenny snapped, at that moment entertaining fantasies of murder. She managed to slide the flimsy material of the suit underneath her body, tying the back with clumsy fingers. As soon as she slid off the raft, Nick scooped her up and set her on the side of the pool, holding her wrist to prevent her from leaving.

"Okay, let's have it," he said, sounding like a resigned martyr.

"Do you have to hold my wrist so tightly? You're cutting off my circulation," Jenny said in the nastiest tone she could muster.

Nick's grip loosened a fraction. Although Jenny was staring out across the pool, she could feel his eyes studying her. Summoning up every bit of control she possessed, she reined in her temper and began a recitation of Nick's sins.

"You followed me down from Davis," she said evenly, proud of the note she had struck—firm but not harsh.

"True," Nick answered laconically, his thumb massaging the inside of her wrist. Jenny resolutely ignored the provocation.

"You put a bug on my car."

"Also true. How else was I going to keep track of you?"

"You lied when you said you'd never met my father," Jenny went on, her voice now strained with pique. She wiggled her wrist impatiently to still Nick's thumb.

"True again. Tell me something I don't know." The subsequent yawn was sheer affectation.

Goaded by Nick's needling, Jenny accused angrily, "The fact is, Mr. Butler, that you and my father are thick as thieves!"

"Now I wouldn't say that. I'd say we have a— pleasant working relationship."

"Right!" Jenny stormed furiously. "You give him money, he does you favors. And let go of my wrist!" She tried to pull away, but Nick simply tightened his grip until it was less painful to stop struggling.

"Not a chance, not until we straighten this out. I'll stop teasing you, although it won't be easy since your reactions are so predictably gratifying," he grinned. "Right now, I'm going to talk and you're going listen, Jenny. And you can save the hostile looks for someone who takes them seriously. Cool down! You're twenty-one, not thirteen." Nick started to stand up, pulling Jenny up along with him. "Into the pool house. It's too hot to sit out here," he ordered.

"Not as hot as where I'd like to see you!" Jenny retorted. With Nick's implication that she was acting like a child, her temper had shifted into high gear. She told herself that she welcomed the opportunity to confront him. He spanked her, teased her, made love to her, lied to her and played juvenile games with her, and when she responded with anger, he told her she was overreacting! Once inside the building, Nick indicated a chair. "Something to drink?" he asked politely.

Jenny shook her head curtly, aching to tell him what he could do with his drink, but telling herself that she had so many justifiable complaints that name-calling was surely unnecessary.

She watched moodily as Nick fixed himself a scotch on the rocks, his motions deft and cool. He strolled over to her, grabbing a chair and positioning it to serve as a footrest, then sprawled back on a love seat. After a healthy swallow of his drink, he began to talk, his voice as smooth as the expensive alcohol in his glass.

"I've known your father for five years. I admire him. His record on business and agriculture is—friendly. I've contributed several thousand dollars to his last few campaigns and I'd like to see him elected governor."

"Tell me something I don't know," Jenny cooed, mimicking Nick's tone of five minutes before.

"You know all that?" Nick's eyebrows arched in surprise as he laughed at her. "You've been a busy little girl. Frankly, honey, I don't see what you're so bent out of shape about. If I hadn't been on such good terms with your father, he never would have let you out of Davis. It was a personal favor to me, nothing more. You're here in Scottsdale, which is what you wanted, so what's the gripe?"

"You honestly *don't* know, do you?" Jenny studied his face, which reflected the nonchalance in his voice. "You—you practically assaulted me in Fresno. You told me one lie after another afterward. It was all a game to you, wasn't it? You let me walk into your mother's home with no idea of who she was or who you were. Didn't it ever occur to you that I might mind? You kissed me—and touched me—in a way that no one ever had before. Didn't you care that I might get hurt?"

Nick merely shook his head impatiently. "Look, Jenny, your father asked me if I could arrange to follow you down and I agreed. I had no intention of your finding out. But you did thousands of dollars worth of damage to a prototype truck, and it wasn't covered by insurance. I wanted to beat the—the tar out of you, and as far as I'm concerned, you deserved it. Afterward, I took a good look at you and decided to combine revenge with a little fun." His lips quirked, then curved upward. "You always rise to the bait, Jenny. I can count on your temper to make you act irrationally, and I doubt very much that I actually hurt you. I apologize if I violated your pristine innocence. But it was only a few kisses and I'm the one who stopped, not you." Laugh lines appeared around his eyes and mouth, his amused tone proclaiming a total lack of repentance.

Jenny sat stunned, feeling a pain start high in her abdomen, just under her ribcage. She was utterly crushed. Was that how Nick Butler classified his passionate lovemaking? As "a few kisses—a little fun"? He must have considered her just a mildly entertaining diversion, not exciting enough to pursue. Little wonder his rejection had been so withering when Jenny had taken his advances seriously. He must have laughed all the way back to his room.

Mustering her pride, Jenny managed to say huskily, "Let me see if I understand this. You justify all the lies by saying I deserved it. You were taking your revenge for the truck. And—and as for kissing me—you . . ." Her voice broke and she stopped, unable to go on.

"Thoroughly enjoyed it," Nick inserted smoothly. "And the rest of what you just said is only partly true.

If I had told you the truth, you might not have come to Scottsdale. And I wanted you to come, because you're young and sweet and lively. You'll be good for Kitty." Nick Butler was no longer smiling. Jenny realized that, at the mention of his daughter, his voice had taken on an urgent, coaxing quality.

Jenny's embarrassment was temporarily forgotten. This was her opportunity to discover more about the child's background. "What do you mean, 'good for Kitty'?" she asked carefully. "Considering what she's been through, she seems—"

"What the devil do you know about what she's been through?" Nick sounded furious. "Don't tell me you've weaseled that out of my mother, too?"

Jenny looked at him in amazement. She was shocked by the abrupt change in his whole demeanor. One moment he had been quite relaxed, although serious, the next moment rigid with anger and aggression. In alluding to Kitty's childhood she had apparently struck a very raw nerve.

"I haven't asked your mother anything," Jenny said quietly, aware that this was no time to challenge Nick.

"Then explain what you meant." He flung himself off the love seat and stalked over to the bar to splash more scotch into his glass. Then he leaned against a stool and stared at Jenny, his eyes wary and his mouth thin with anger.

Jenny took a deep breath, wishing there were some way to stall. Then she decided it would be better to get it over with. "The first day I met Kitty, she expressed—doubts that she was really your daughter. She told me that your wife—"

"Ex-wife," Nick cut in curtly.

"Ex-wife," Jenny inserted the correction, "wouldn't

let your mother and stepfather visit her in California. She feels terribly guilty over her mother's death, as if she could have saved her. And several times she's mentioned different men friends, as if your—ex-wife changed them pretty often. If your marriage was anything like your divorce, it must have been—"

"It's none of your damn business," Nick growled furiously. "You weren't hired as a social worker, *Miss* Ross."

Having come this far, Jenny was not about to back off. Timidity was not one of her faults. "You say I'd be good for Kitty," she persisted. "How am I supposed to help a child who's obviously traumatized if—"

"Damn it, I told you it's none of your business! Marcia died in a boating accident. Kitty was at a movie with me at the time so she could hardly be responsible. *Naturally* her mother's death traumatized her. That's all you need to know." Each word was bitten off and flung out, the sentences punctuated by sips of scotch.

Jenny's heart was pounding fiercely, the verbal attack stimulating her adrenaline as effectively as the threat of violence would have. There was an uncomfortable silence, Jenny staring at the floor while Nick finished his drink. Once her blood pressure had returned to normal, Jenny decided to pursue a safer topic of conversation. She murmured, "Kitty is intelligent, sweet and helpful. Fortunately for all of us, I work for your mother, so if you and I don't get along, we—"

"Whatever gave you that idea?"

Jenny's eyes flew up to meet Nick's. He was once again in control of his emotions, his body lazing indolently against the stool, his tone dry. "Wh— what?" she asked uncertainly.

"You don't work for my mother. You work for me. I

wanted someone young and energetic to take care of Kitty. The only reason you don't live here is because I'm thirty-three and single and people would make assumptions. The arrangement suits *my* convenience, and *I* pay the bills."

Even in the desert heat, this piece of information made Jenny shiver. If it hadn't been such a struggle to escape her father's domination, she would have begun packing that very afternoon. She hated the thought of being subject to Nick Butler's authority. She felt trapped.

"You understand the situation now?" Nick's voice seemed to come from very far off. Jenny nodded.

"Don't look so stricken," Nick gibed. "Most of the time you'll be dealing with my mother. But when I tell you to do something, I don't want arguments and back talk. I'm the boss. And if you know what's good for you, you'll remember that."

Jenny slowly turned her head to focus on Nick, warmth flooding back into her body. His head was tilted back, his features composed into an arrogant mask. She knew perfectly well what he was doing. Nick Butler was far too confident and self-assured to bother reminding his subordinates that he was in charge. Five minutes in the same room with him and no one could fail to know it. His outrageously dominating attitude was calculated to make her explode with resentment. It seemed to amuse him.

Although Jenny was powerless to control the spark of temper that Nick's attitude ignited, she refused to give him satisfaction by losing her temper yet again. She stood up, fixed contemptuous brown eyes on him, and said acidly, "Yes sir, Mr. Butler. What are my orders, sir?"

Nick only smiled at the sarcasm. "My mother and Oscar are celebrating their tenth anniversary two weeks from Sunday. I'm having a surprise party for them Saturday night." He took several steps forward to grasp Jenny's arm and lead her out of the pool house, a gesture she tolerated with stiff dislike. "I have a list of things I'd like you to take care of for me, Jenny," he told her.

When she made no reply, he firmly tipped her chin up with his finger, forcing her to look at him. "Don't look so disapproving, honey. I know the party isn't your job, but I'd appreciate your help. Please." His soft tone was all silky persuasion.

Nick's closeness and coaxing had a very potent physical effect on Jenny, and she was sure he knew it. Nonetheless, self-preservation dictated that she resist the man's appeal. "Why of course," she answered sweetly. "I'd be delighted to help in any way I can, Mr. Butler. Your mother and stepfather are such warm, thoughtful people."

"Meaning I'm not," Nick grinned, putting his arm around Jenny's shoulder to gently push her toward the house.

They entered through the living room, which was furnished with off-white sectional seating grouped around a massive stone fireplace. Several Navajo rugs were scattered on the polished parquet floor. The redwood shelving on either side of the fireplace appeared to have been custom-built to house Nick's collection of Indian artwork. Jenny stared at the pottery and paintings, entranced. She recognized several red and buff Hohokan pieces, probably over a thousand years old; there were numerous other tribes represented, including Hopi jars and Jenny's personal favorites, the black-on-black vases and pots of San Ildefonso, New Mexico.

One shelf, enclosed in glass, held a collection of Zuni and Hopi Kachina dolls, colorful and bizarre figures depicting warriors, animals and Indian deities. Several primitive sculptures also graced the shelves, and displayed around the room was a dazzling array of Native American art, most of the paintings stylized or abstract. The colors stood out boldly against the neutral tones of the furniture, walls and floor.

Jennys' eyes were glowing with pleasure by the time she turned back to Nick. "This room is beautiful. Now I understand why you put up the fence."

Nick made no reply, but took Jenny's arm and led her to the dining room, which was an L-shaped extension off the living room. He pointed to two waist-high pedestals holding fearsome looking stone figures. "Pre-Columbian, and well worth stealing." The ancient sculptures contrasted strikingly with the modern, glass-topped dining table.

They walked down several steps, crossed the kitchen and entered a breakfast room where Nick motioned Jenny into a chair. Then, noting that she was absent-mindedly rubbing her arms, he went to fetch her a shirt, which she gratefully accepted. He had pulled on a short-sleeved tennis shirt.

"I looked in on Kitty. She's still asleep, fortunately." Jenny regarded him quizzically and he continued, "The child's a sieve. If she knew about the surprise party, it wouldn't remain a surprise. I don't know how you're going to do it, but see that she doesn't find out."

Nick handed her a pencil and notepad and reeled off

a long list of instructions, concerning such things as the guest list, liquor and soft drinks, bartenders, the band and the caterers. His voice was cool, as though Jenny was one of his junior secretaries. The earlier coaxing charm was gone, switched off because he no longer needed it. Jenny suddenly realized that Nick had brought her into the house because he knew his collection of Indian artifacts would please her into cooperating. She resented the manipulation. "Aren't you afraid I'll mess things up?" she asked coldly.

"Not at all. I figure it's in the genes. Your grandmother is famous for her parties, and a little of it should have rubbed off. You'll do fine."

"What do you know about my grandmother's parties?" Jenny had been to more of these affairs than she cared to remember. They tended to include many of the same people over and over again. In Jenny's opinion, too many of them were either boring or offensively lecherous.

"I've been to a few of them," Nick told her. "The most recent, about six months ago. You were there, but at the time I had no idea you were Emerson's daughter. I couldn't stay long enough to meet you."

"A pity," Jenny interjected sourly.

"You were wearing a black strapless dress, and you looked sensational." Jenny cursed her tendency to blush so easily, because her reaction seemed to encourage Nick to tease her. "I was with a date, and we were on our way to the theater. Otherwise I would have introduced myself."

"And waited for me to genuflect?" Jenny asked acidly.

"And waited for you to fall into my arms, which,

judging by your reaction in Bakersfield and Indio, is exactly what you would have done."

Jenny considered it nasty but typical of Nick to remind her of something so embarrassing, especially in the mocking tone he was using. "That was before I knew what a skunk you are," she said, as haughtily as she could. To her dismay, Nick simply shook his head reprovingly.

Their verbal battle was terminated by the sound of a piercing wail. Nick bolted out of his chair; Jenny followed him back through the house to Kitty's room. His daughter was lying on top of the covers, her tangled hair and flushed face damp with perspiration, her eyes wet with tears. As Jenny watched from the doorway, Nick gathered her into his arms to comfort her. "Oh Daddy," she moaned, "I was on the boat, and the wind was blowing . . ."

Nick rocked her gently back and forth, stroking her hair and murmuring to her in a low, soothing voice. Jenny couldn't make out his words. When Kitty's sobs had tapered off to an occasional hiccuping whimper, Nick began to tell her an amusing story about something that had happened in Tucson. Soon she was laughing with delight, her nightmare temporarily forgotten.

Suddenly the child seemed to remember Jenny's presence. Her cheeks dimpled with pleasure as she told her father, "I'm so glad you came home early. And you've met Jenny. Isn't she pretty?"

"Very. Almost as beautiful as you are, kitten." He ruffled her hair. "I'm getting hungry. Let's go to Grandma's."

Jenny volunteered to gather their clothing and towels

from the pool, walking through the master bedroom to the patio. A huge waterbed, stone fireplace and warm, sensuous artwork—some of the pictures were nudes—gave the room an embarrassingly voluptuous feel. She was relieved to step outside to fetch their belongings.

Kitty and her father were waiting in the hall. As the three of them stepped outside, Nick held out his hand. "I took a cab from the airport. Give me your car keys, Jenny."

Jenny knew that an expensive sports car and a Rolls Royce were sitting side by side in the garage, but she had no desire to enter into yet another argument with Nick. She docilely handed him the keys and opened the passenger door.

"How are we going to get back, Daddy?" Kitty was nestled between the two adults in the front seat.

"Jenny will drive us." Nick glanced at her mutinous expression as he drove down the driveway. "Or Grandpa," he added with a chuckle.

The minute Jenny walked through the door, she realized how difficult the next few hours would be. The Hermanns greeted Nick with delight and warmth, prompting Jenny to think to herself that he might have returned from an expedition up the Nile for all the fuss they were making. Dinner was already in the oven; Mrs. Hermann shepherded everyone into the living room for cocktails and conversation.

Dr. Hermann was in the middle of an amusing anecdote when the phone rang. Mrs. Hermann rose to answer it, returning a moment later to tell Jenny it was her father and suggesting that she take the call in the den. She was surprised to find that she was actually glad he had called. She had missed him, just a little bit.

"Hi, Dad," she said cheerfully. "How's the campaign going?" It was Jenny's idea of a joke; Emerson Ross hadn't had any serious opposition since his second term in office.

He ignored her attempt at humor. "We've been expecting a call from you, Jennifer."

"But I spoke to Emiko on Saturday. Didn't you get the message that I'd arrived safely?" Jenny protested.

"Naturally. Nick phoned as well. But we expected you would call back when you didn't reach us, darling."

Jenny felt that he was being totally unreasonable. Surely it was more logical for her parents to call her than for Jenny to make long distance calls from the Hermanns' phone. But she knew there was no point arguing. "I'm sorry if you were concerned, Dad," she said with a sigh. "But I'm fine. Kitty—the little girl—is very sweet. And the Hermanns have been very nice to me. How are you and Mom? Busy?"

"I understand you wrecked Nick's truck."

Jenny's temper began to simmer. She wondered sourly if Nick had turned in a detailed report on her misdeeds. Rather than make a comment she would regret, she said nothing.

"You're lucky it happened to be his," Emerson Ross continued in a quietly disapproving tone. "You left the scene of an accident. That's against the law, Jennifer. You could have found yourself in serious trouble."

"He deserved it!" Jenny spat out. "He was going 65 coming onto the freeway, and—"

"It's fortunate he spent the rest of the trip keeping an eye on you, Jennifer. If I didn't have Nick's word that he would take care of you, I'd put Emiko on the next plane to Phoenix to fetch you back here."

Emiko! Of course, you couldn't be bothered to come yourself, Jenny thought furiously. As for Nicholas J. Butler, his behavior was despicable. How *could* he have told her father what had happened?

"I assumed you would stay out of trouble, Jennifer. I wouldn't have agreed to let you go to Scottsdale if I had realized—"

"And what else did Nick tell you?" Jenny interrupted, her tongue loosened by fury. "Did he tell you he practically seduced me in the swimming pool in Indio?" The moment the words were out, she closed her eyes, clenched her fists, and winced with regret. When would she learn to control herself?

"Put him on the phone, Jennifer." Her father's voice was cold with anger.

"Look, Dad, it wasn't really that bad." Jenny tried desperately to placate him. "He kissed me a few times, that's all. You know how I exaggerate when I'm angry."

"Now, Jennifer."

With a shrug of resignation, Jenny went back to the living room to fetch Nick. The longer she stalled her father, the angrier he would become.

"My father would like to talk to you," she said to Nick in a stilted voice. He put down his scotch and walked over to her, his eyebrows raised in inquiry. When they were alone in the hall, Jenny added awkwardly, "We were having an argument. I got angry because he knew about the truck, and I told him—you—you—"

"I get the picture," Nick said, quite unconcerned by that fact. He picked up the phone and drawled, "Hello, Mr. Speaker. What can I do for you?"

There was silence in the room for a full minute. As Nick listened, he leaned against the desk, apparently unaffected by the tirade Jenny assumed was assaulting his right ear. Finally he replied coolly, "Your daughter is very beautiful, Emerson. Also very hot-tempered. It's an explosive combination, and I'm not immune to it. But I promise you, if I seduce her, I'll marry her."

"Don't do me any favors," Jenny hissed fiercely. Nick had begun to laugh softly, apparently at something her father was telling him.

"Right. I appreciate it, Emerson," There was a pause. "No, I don't think I should do that. Good-bye." He turned to Jenny, who glared up at him, her face red with embarrassment and anger. "He told me to give you a kiss from him. But you don't look too receptive at the moment." Without another word, he strolled out the door.

Jenny threw herself into the desk chair and tried to calm down. Her father had been enraged with Nick Butler, and yet just a few well-chosen words from that egotistical brute had dispelled his black mood. They had obviously said good-bye on the friendliest of terms. As matters stood now, her father would probably be delighted if Nick seduced her. He found the man a highly acceptable future son-in-law. Jenny's thoughts consigned both domineering males to the most fiery of places, preferably in each other's company.

Most of the mealtime conversation concerned the results of Nick's most recent business trip, and Jenny was unable to prevent her temper from boiling out of control. After Nick commented that the mining company he had acquired had a poor health and safety record, Jenny asked sarcastically, "And is AMT any better?"

Mrs. Hermann looked appalled at the accusation, but Nick simply answered evenly, "Yes, we're better. You're welcome to check with the feds, Miss Ross."

Jenny contented herself with a saccharine, "Oh no, Mr. Butler, I'll take your word for it. After all, I have no reason to think you would lie to me, do I?"

Nick's no was extremely curt and, mercifully, Oscar Hermann changed the subject. Jenny, aware that she was alienating Mrs. Hermann, vowed to keep a tight rein on her temper. She knew that if she continued to let her resentment flare out of control, she would find herself unemployed. Mrs. Hermann was obviously shocked by her behavior, and Nick's stony expression showed his annoyance all too clearly. Worst of all, Kitty looked baffled and hurt because two people she cared for weren't getting along. Only Dr. Hermann showed no negative reaction, and Jenny suspected that he had reasoned out the cause of her sarcastic comments.

After dinner, the adults retired to the living room to talk while Kitty went into the den to watch TV. The conversation was innocuous and Jenny was able to participate in a civil manner. Apparently reassured, Mrs. Hermann broached the subject of arrangements for the next several days, hesitantly telling her son, "Jenny is willing to come make dinner for you and Kitty, if you want her to."

"That depends." Nick's harsh stare dissected Jenny. "Do you think you can manage to stop trying to score points? It upsets Kitty."

"Do you think you can manage to . . ." Jenny forced back the rest of the sentence—"keep your hands off me"—in favor of a tight little pause and a curt, "I'll do my best, *sir*." At that moment, she felt she could not endure another minute of Nicholas Butler's company. She abruptly excused herself, not caring that Marian Hermann was regarding her with extreme disapproval.

Oscar Hermann drove Nick and Kitty home, which left Jenny alone in the house with Mrs. Hermann. She greeted the knock on her door with a sigh of resignation.

"I'll come straight to the point," Mrs. Hermann said bluntly. "When you left the room this evening, I suggested to Nicholas that we send you back to California. He told me that you had good reason to be angry with him and rather forcefully suggested that I mind my own business. It's clear that there are many things I'm not privy to, Jenny, and I've learned to stay out of my son's personal affairs. But I must insist that when you're in my house, you control your temper. I found your comment about our company more objectionable than I can tell you."

The dressing down made Jenny thoroughly ashamed of her outbursts. AMT was as much Mrs. Hermann's company as her son's; she had been appallingly rude to a woman who had shown her nothing but kindness and consideration.

"I'm—I'm sorry, Mrs. Hermann," she mumbled, forcing herself to meet the other woman's eyes. "I won't—I'll try—" To Jenny's utter consternation, she burst into tears.

The next moment she was sobbing uncontrollably on Mrs. Hermann's shoulder and feeling a relief and comfort she had never experienced with her coolly elegant mother, Jacqueline. But as much as she needed someone to confide in, she could not bring herself to discuss Nick Butler with his mother. Mrs. Hermann seemed instinctively to understand this. When Jenny had disentangled herself and was calm enough to listen, she said soothingly, "Nicholas can be difficult, I know that, Jenny. Just remember, I'm here if you need me." And in a thoroughly natural maternal gesture, she leaned over and kissed Jenny good-night.

Chapter Six

Jenny's verbal battles with her parents usually lasted only a few minutes; the subsequent cold wars had a habit of dragging on for days. Even after the requisite apologies and filial kisses, her mother and father often continued to punish her with a cool manner and even cooler silences.

Thus, when she emerged from her room for breakfast Thursday morning, she was unsure of her reception. The Hermanns were sitting at the kitchen table drinking coffee and reading the newspaper; Jenny's "Good morning" was tentative, her smile uncertain.

"Good morning, Jenny. Have you recovered sufficiently from the ordeal of dealing with my stepson to have some breakfast this morning?" Dr. Hermann folded the paper neatly as he spoke, his voice gently teasing.

Marian finished her coffee and carried the empty

mug to the sink, shaking her head in pretended exasperation with her husband. "Really, Oscar! One impossible man in Jenny's life is more than enough. Can I trust you to behave yourself if I leave to finish dressing?" To Jenny she added, "Try to eat something, dear. Nick should be dropping Kitty off any minute now."

She poured herself some grapefruit juice and put a slice of whole wheat bread into the toaster oven. Jenny was aware that Dr. Hermann was following her movements with amused eyes. "Honestly, Dr. Hermann," she said, "you should have been a biologist instead of a humanities professor."

"And why is that, Jenny?" His lips quirked into a smile.

"Because you've been staring at me as though you'd like to dissect me!" Jenny knew what was on his mind. "Go ahead, ask me. I'll survive."

"Marian would disapprove, you know," he said with feigned solemnity. "As would Nicholas. But I have a most analytical mind, Jenny. Based upon observation, I have concluded that you met my stepson prior to yesterday afternoon, probably on the way to Scottsdale. But I believe you had no knowledge of his identity. Am I correct?"

The man's ability to extrapolate was incredible! Jenny busied herself with spreading butter on her toast and admitted, "Yes, you're right about everything. But how did you know? Did Nick tell you about it?"

There was a roar of laughter from Oscar. "My dear Jenny, if Nicholas had told me about it, I'd not have to ask you, would I?"

Jenny shook her head and carried her toast and juice to the table. She wasn't surprised that Nick had told his stepfather nothing. He wasn't the type of man to discuss his private affairs, even with his family.

Apparently satisfied, Dr. Hermann began to ask Jenny about her experiences at college, suggesting to her that she might take a course or two at his school, and eventually earn her degree. Her contact with Dr. Hermann had made Jenny realize that formal education was not necessarily as boring as she had assumed, and she accepted his offer to bring her a fall catalogue.

Their conversation was interrupted by the sound of a car pulling up in front of the house. Jenny answered the door just as Kitty was about to ring the bell; Nick was sitting sideways in the bucket seat of his sports car, watching them. His eyes met Jenny's for a fleeting moment before he gunned the accelerator and pulled out into the street.

Kitty had not yet eaten breakfast, so Jenny made her some French toast. As the child ate, Jenny suggested that they spend the morning taking stock of her father's larder, then go shopping for whatever he needed. Kitty wrinkled her nose. "We can skip the first part. We have some juice, a stick of butter, half a carton of milk, wilted lettuce and a bunch of stuff wrapped up in foil."

Nonetheless, Jenny insisted on a thorough inventory, which resulted in a two-page shopping list, including many items added at Kitty's request. Just as Jenny was wondering how she was going to pay for all the food, Kitty produced an envelope containing ten twenty dollar bills. "Daddy said to give you this," she explained. "Is there enough money?"

"Unless inflation's skyrocketed overnight, I think we'll manage," Jenny joked.

Their foray to the supermarket and butcher took an hour and a half. They returned with eleven well-packed brown bags to find a pickup truck parked in front of the house. Kitty told Jenny it belonged to the housekeeper, who had her own set of keys to the gate and house.

Her name was Mary, and she appeared to be only a few years older than Jenny. It was obvious from her black hair and facial structure that she was part Indian, and soon the two young women were comparing notes on their ancestry.

Jenny had once visited her distant relatives on a Navajo reservation in New Mexico, but had felt out of place and uncomfortable among these nomadic shepherd cousins. It was her grandmother Silver Moon who had given her an understanding and appreciation of how her Indian heritage related to twentieth century American life. Jenny had a great feeling for nature, considerable talent as a silversmith, and the opportunity to contribute something to her people in her way.

She was Emerson Ross's daughter and he was an influential man. Whenever legislation was introduced concerning California's Native American population, Jenny would talk to her father about it. Sometimes he accepted her point of view; more often he simply tolerated her lectures. It was the one area where she refused to be intimidated or sidetracked, however, and Emerson Ross supported the Indian point of view more often than he could normally have been expected to. His wife Jacqueline was thought to be responsible.

Recently, Jenny had read of a complaint filed by a southern California tribe against a large chemical company. The tribe claimed the company was polluting its lands; the company denied it. Jenny made a visit to her grandfather in San Francisco, correctly assuming that he would have contacts in the powerful Los Angeles firm representing the chemical company. A phone call to the surprised tribal chief had procured a ream of documents; the man was delighted that Emerson Ross's daughter wanted to help.

Emerson Ross, Sr. was not particularly enthusiastic about his granddaughter's identification with her Indian grandmother, but she was his only grandchild and he adored her in spite of her quirks. He listened to her argument, was impressed by it, and promised he would do what he could.

She never knew whom he called or what he said, only that the chemical company settled out of court, to the tribe's ultimate satisfaction.

When Jenny told Mary something of her background, Mary immediately asked about the jewelry she crafted. She explained that she also worked for a couple named Mr. and Mrs. Barber who owned an Indian crafts store and workshop/school in Scottsdale. At Jenny's request, she wrote the store's address on a piece of paper, and Jenny promised to call on them.

It had taken over an hour to put away the groceries because Jenny and Mary had decided to clean the shelves and rearrange the food. Afterward, they sat down over a cup of coffee and Kitty went off to her room to read.

The few minutes' break Mary had allowed herself had stretched to half an hour when Mary glanced at the kitchen wall clock and gasped, "I've got to go back to work. Mr. Butler pays me by the hour."

"He can spare the money." Jenny hadn't meant the comment to come out quite so acidly and was relieved that Kitty hadn't been there to hear it. Mary seemed shocked by Jenny's sarcasm.

"He's very generous. He wanted to pay me by the week, but some days there's so little to do that it wouldn't be fair. He gives me more than I asked for. He says I work fast and do a good job, and I'm worth it. And he never gets angry if my son is sick and I can't come." Her voice was earnest to the point of adulation.

Jenny had noticed the plain gold band on Mary's finger. "You're married then? What does your husband do?"

"He works for Mr. Butler's trucking company. Mr. Butler is a wonderful boss. If we're all done in here . . . ?" She waited for Jenny's nod, then went back to work.

It seemed to Jenny that Nicholas Butler's employees thought very highly of him, and for the first time she admitted to herself that the man probably had a positive side. She went off in search of Kitty, and although the child was immersed in an electronic game she was happy to put it aside in favor of baking some chocolate chip cookies with Jenny. Afterward, Kitty helped to bone chicken and clean shrimp for dinner.

Mary declined Jenny's offer of lunch, saying she had another job to go to. During the rest of the afternoon, Kitty and Jenny lazed in the pool, but this time Jenny kept her suit firmly in place. She swam laps with Kitty in a fruitless effort to keep her mind away from the question of how she would react when she saw Nick later in the day.

At the Hermann's understanding forgiveness of Jenny's sarcasm, she had felt a definite internal change. For as long as she could remember, she had struggled with her parents for the right to have her own identity. They had been determined to turn her into a *soigné* San Francisco socialite and she had been just as determined to resist. She was beginning to realize just how much it had cost her to constantly rebel against their wishes. A good deal of the tension, anger and quick temper she often exhibited had its roots in the fact that she was engaged in a protracted war.

Now she was living with two people who seemed to take an interest in Jennifer Ross as an individual, not as a symbol or a way to get to her father, and Jenny was unusually relaxed and amenable in their presence. Nick Butler, of course, was another proposition. She considered him to be a younger version of her father, and whenever she was in the same room with him she felt a childish urge to demonstrate her independence. Often this took the form of challenging him when there was no real reason to do so. His pompous promise to her father that he would marry her if he seduced her was a further source of irritation.

But in spite of this tempestuous reaction to Nick, the greater part of Jenny's energy was no longer sapped by stubborn resistance and blazing arguments. As a result, she felt capable of remaining civil in Nick's presence, and hoped her self-congratulations wouldn't prove premature.

Fortunately for Jenny, it seemed that Nick had decided not to put her new found self-control to the test. She had just finished preparations for dinner and was waiting for Nick to come home before actually cooking the food when Kitty came in from the den to say she had seen his car coming up the drive.

A moment later Nick walked in, picking Kitty up to kiss her. She greeted him enthusiastically, then scampered off to watch the rest of a TV show. Jenny half-expected Nick to bestow a mocking kiss on her as well, but he limited himself to an investigation of the dinner.

"I've had a rotten day. I shouldn't have stayed away

from the office for so long." He nodded toward the breaded shrimp and vegetables. "Japanese food?"

"Tempura," Jenny said, "and there's teriyaki marinating in the fridge. Are you hungry?"

"Starved. I didn't get a chance to eat lunch. Also thirsty." He opened a cabinet above the counter, then frowned at the cereal and other staples inside. "Where's the liquor?"

"We rearranged things. It's in the cabinet above the counter between the kitchen and the breakfast room." Jenny made a vague motion with her right hand. "We sorted through and only kept one of everything. You had a dozen bottles of flat mixers and five bottles half full of scotch in there."

"Jenny, you didn't pour the Chivas Regal into the Dewar's, did you?" Nick questioned in mock horror. Jenny merely shook her head, rolled her eyes, and started to deep-fry the tempura. Meanwhile, Nick poked around in the cabinets, ascertaining the new locations of the food. Then he poured himself a Scotch and leaned against the counter to watch Jenny cook. "Been busy today, hmm? There's enough food in this house to feed the entire office staff of AMT."

"You said you were hungry," Jenny retorted. A glass cookie jar filled with Kitty's chocolate chip cookies rested on the counter and Nick opened it, snatched out a cookie, and devoured it in two bites. Then he took out a second, finishing it just as rapidly.

"Don't say it," he ordered in response to Jenny's disapproving look. "I told you, I'm starved. I'll finish whatever you make, believe me."

And he did. Jenny was pleased that everything tasted perfect, even though she was a good cook and expected delicious results. Dinner conversation was noncontroversial and surprisingly pleasant. Images of herself as Nick's wife flashed through Jenny's mind from time to time; she could feel herself blush as thoughts of the kitchen gave way to thoughts of the bedroom. When she wasn't furious with Nick Butler, she found him undeniably attractive. Lazing back in his chair, sipping his coffee, he was dazzling.

He must have guessed her thoughts, because when she glanced at him he was smiling rather wickedly at her. "How about bringing those cookies in here, Kitty?" he said to his daughter, who willingly obliged.

To Jenny he added, "I'm not such an ogre after all, hmm?" His smile was so charmingly crooked that her heartbeat accelerated sharply. She could feel her nipples tauten under the t-shirt she wore, and was relieved that her bikini top hid her body's betrayal from Nick's eyes.

"I'm delighted to learn that you can be civil, Mr. Butler. Is this a one-night stand, or can you manage it tomorrow night also?" Although there was an edge to the words, her tone was huskily flirtatious. Her thoughts drifted back to the meal she and Nick had shared in Indio, and Jenny felt the same powerful emotional tug she had experienced that evening.

Nick answered the question just as Kitty was returning with the cookies. "We won't be eating dinner here tomorrow. We'll be eating at a friend's house."

"What friend?" This from Kitty, who spoke the words with her mouth full of cookies.

"The Templetons."

Nick's tone was unusually curt and Jenny soon understood why. At the mention of their hosts' name, Kitty burst out, "Ugh! I'm not going *there*. I'm staying with Jenny."

"You're going and that's final. Finish your dinner."

"I already finished my dinner. Can't you see that? This is dessert. And I'm not going to the Templetons." Jenny had never heard such a cheeky tone from Kitty, and judging from her father's strained expression he had no intention of letting her get away with it.

"It isn't open to argument, Nichole. First you'll apologize for your rudeness, then you'll go to bed." Jenny sensed that Nick was controlling his anger only with great difficulty.

"I can't stand Joanna. She always acts like she's so glad to see me, but she's a phony. She hates kids—she even left Joey. She's awful!" Kitty glared at her father. "And I won't say I'm sorry. I'm not!"

Nick muttered an impatient curse and scraped back his chair to stand up. By the time he rose, Kitty had already flung herself out of her chair and was running toward her room. Her father strode after her, his expression grim.

Jenny heard a wail from down the hall. She cleared the table to the accompaniment of the girl's loud sobbing. Then there was a protracted silence.

By the time Nick and Kitty reemerged, Jenny had finished cleaning up the kitchen and was debating whether or not to interrupt them to say she was leaving.

Father and daughter stood side by side, framed in the doorway. After a stern look from Nick, Kitty mumbled, "I'm sorry, Jenny. Good-night." She looked thoroughly miserable.

Jenny knew she mustn't challenge Nick's parental decisions. His eyes were icy as he waited for her reaction to Kitty's apology, almost as if he were daring her to defy his judgment. As tempted as she was, she knew there was a limit to how much she could antagonize him, he was, after all, her boss, and get away with it. She contented herself with a disapproving glare at Nick and then bent down to kiss Kitty good-night. "It's okay, honey. I'll see you in the morning."

With her head drooping, Kitty slunk out of the kitchen, just as though her father were an emperor who had banished her to the outer provinces. Jenny was about to collect her purse from the counter when Nick said coldly, "Thank you for making dinner, Jenny. You can go now."

His lord of the manor attitude destroyed what remained of her self-control. "Don't use that tone of voice on me," she snapped. "I'm not ten years old!"

"Then don't act like it. I've had enough tantrums for one night. Get moving!" He turned his back to her and started to leave the kitchen.

"No wonder Kitty has problems," Jenny spat out, furious with him for his offensive mode of dismissal. "You act like a dictator. Why don't you talk to her instead of bossing her around? She's your daughter, not your slave!"

Nick slowly turned. There was no mistaking his reaction to Jenny's criticism—he was livid. "I'll remind you of your position here, Miss Ross. You work for me. You do what I tell you. If you can't manage that, get out."

A chill shuddered through Jenny's body and she stood rooted to the floor, astonished at her own vehemence. Why was she becoming so emotional about the scene she had witnessed? Nick was right; it *was* none of her business. She should apologize and walk out the door.

But she couldn't. She identified with Kitty. She

remembered too many similar scenes at her own dinner table, scenes when her father had ridden roughshod over her feelings and forced her to accede to his wishes. There were never any explanations or discussions, only orders. She had grown too fond of Kitty to let the matter drop, even if it meant leaving Scottsdale.

"All right," she said calmly, no longer tense or angry because she felt she was doing the right thing. "I'll leave as soon as you can replace me. But I remember what it feels like to be ten years old and have a father make me do things I hated. If he had only taken the time to talk to me . . . but he never did." She picked up her purse and slung it over her shoulder. "I know you love Kitty. I hope you'll realize you can't treat her the way you did tonight and have her continue to return that love. If she has fears and doubts, help her with them."

Jenny was halfway to the front door before Nick's hand closed around her upper arm. "Into the living room. We have some talking to do."

She didn't argue. She was suddenly very relieved that Nick Butler wasn't letting her walk out of his life.

He pulled her down on the couch, sitting some distance away from her. "First," he said in a soft, angry voice, "I resent sitting here and giving you explanations. I'm doing it because Kitty would be unhappy if you left. But damn it, Jenny, don't expect me to make a habit of it."

Heaven forbid! Jenny thought to herself. But she said nothing, simply stared straight ahead, her expression resentful.

"The minute Kitty and I came back into the kitchen, you looked at me like I was some kind of child abuser.

Don't judge me, Jenny, especially when you don't have the facts."

"And what are the facts?"

"Kitty isn't you, and I'm not your father," Nick continued more gently. "Why do you think I spent twenty minutes in her room? To whip her into shape? She's not used to seeing me with other women. I was reassuring her. Part of the reason she dislikes Joanna is because she's afraid she's going to wake up some morning and find herself with a stepmother. As long as Joanna is just—a good friend—Kitty doesn't mind going to the Templetons. In fact, she's crazy about the old man, Joanna's father, the Senator. I explained to Kitty that I wouldn't remarry until both of us were ready for it. That won't be for a long time. Now are you satisfied that I'm a fit parent?"

Jenny stared blindly in front of her, feeling a familiar stabbing pain under her ribcage. So Nick intended to marry this Joanna Templeton, certainly not immediately, but eventually. The idea of it was insupportable, agonizing. Jenny had no idea how wounded she looked as she sat there, immersed in her own thoughts.

"Jenny?"

She felt unbearably awkward, her only thought to get out of the house without making a total fool of herself. "I'm sorry," she managed in a husky voice. Nick's face wore a grim frown, and suddenly Jenny wanted to beg him not to look at her with such crushing dislike.

Nick stood up; Jenny, interpreting it as a signal that he was through with her, rose and walked out of the room ahead of him. She was much too absorbed in her unhappiness to remember the triple step that divided the living room from the hall.

She stumbled and fell forward, and only Nick's hands on her waist prevented her from sprawling to the floor. The next moment one hand was lifting her chin and the other was around her back, turning her around and pulling her close. For an agonizing moment Nick stood motionless, his icy blue eyes studying her vulnerable brown ones. Then he cursed softly and brushed his mouth over hers.

Jenny, knowing that she should pull away but unable to do so, closed her eyes and tried not to tremble. She felt a lingering kiss at the corner of her mouth; then the point of his tongue traced the outline of her lower lip while his hand left her chin to slip under her shirt and move silkily across her breast.

As before, Jenny found the deliberateness of Nick's approach unbearably exciting. She knew he was teasing her, making her ache to feel his mouth on hers.

His mouth made a thorough tour of her neck, nibbling in a painfully gentle way that left Jenny breathless with longing. By the time he raised his head to take possession of her slightly parted lips, he could have picked her up and carried her into his bedroom and she wouldn't have uttered a single protest, despite the knowledge that he was only using her as a substitute for Joanna Templeton.

At first the kiss was seductive and lazy, Nick's hold on her no more than firm. Jenny twined one arm around his neck and rested the other at his waist, letting it slide down to stroke the side of his muscled leg. She responded with her whole body, moving against him provocatively, the nails of her hand digging into his shoulder.

Nick's hold tightened; his mouth forced her lips further apart in a kiss that became progressively deeper, rougher and more demandingly passionate. Abruptly, he picked her up, his mouth still ravishing hers, and started down the hall.

They had just passed the den when he jerked his head away and, breathing raggedly, turned on his heel and carried her back to the front door. He gently set her on her feet, silencing her confused protest by placing a finger against her lips.

"Jenny, my nine year old daughter is lying in bed a few yards down the hall." Jenny had been so dizzy with arousal that she had completely forgotten Kitty's presence. Given Kitty's fear that Nick would remarry, she would have been terribly upset if she had seen them kissing. The thought made Jenny go pale with guilt.

"But even if she wasn't," Nick went on evenly, "this shouldn't have happened. I'm sorry, Jenny."

The apology stung. Jenny took it as a verbal rejection, and somehow this was even worse than his previous physical rejection. Then she understood exactly what he was saying and her face flushed with embarrassment.

"Of course you're sorry," she choked out. "I nearly forgot, if we had—had made love, you would have had to *marry* me! Poor Joanna!"

"Joanna has nothing to do with it!"

"And your promise to my father?" Jenny asked, not believing him. "Does that have nothing to do with it, too?"

For a long moment Nick simply stared at her. Then he closed his eyes and shook his head, exasperated. "I had a lousy first marriage. I don't want to marry again. But all that's beside the point. You're twenty-one years old, Jenny. You're a virgin. You work for me. Even if I hadn't promised Emerson anything, I still wouldn't make love to you. I never should have laid a hand on you in the first place, and if it happens again . . ." Nick shook his head again, and when he continued, his tone was self-deprecating. "I seem to have a problem keeping my hands off you, and it's obvious that you'll let me do anything I want. That leaves two solutions. Either you stop working for me or I make sure that we're not alone together. Believe it or not, I want Kitty to be happy. Since she likes you so much, we can strike the first option . . ." He opened the front door and firmly pushed Jenny out into the night.

Jenny told herself that it was for the best. She told herself at ten o'clock and twelve o'clock and two o'clock. And when she woke up the next morning, she told herself all over again.

She thought with resignation that even if Nick changed his mind about remarriage, it wouldn't be because of her. Although he was strongly attracted to her, he found her impossibly volatile and childish. Since he had no interest in a serious relationship, she should be grateful that he was honorable enough to keep his distance. But she wasn't. The thought that he would never hold her or kiss her again was as painful as anything she had ever experienced. The phrase "just good friends" usually meant that people were a good deal more than that, and Jenny was achingly jealous of Joanna Templeton.

She admitted to herself that the suspicion, anger and resentment she felt toward Nick had never really diminished his attraction for her. When they weren't arguing, she very much enjoyed his company. In addition, she continued to find his physical appeal embarrassingly irresistible. But now that she knew more about him, new emotions were surfacing. He had looked so tired before dinner; he probably worked too hard. If Kitty's outburst had angered him, it had also upset him deeply. His brief allusions to his first marriage were filled with bitterness, but also with pain. She wanted to take care of him. She wanted to ease the hurt and bitterness. She wanted Nick to take her seriously.

And when Jenny wanted something badly enough, she fought to have it. In her own way, she realized, she could be just as willful and persistent as her father. She told herself that there were two ways to get what she wanted. The first was to trap Nick into bed and marriage. There was only one problem with this scenario: he would never forgive her.

Her second option was more difficult: she would have to grow up a great deal. No more temper tantrums, no more acid criticism, no more wild accusations. Nick already found her appealing; perhaps she could make him feel a great deal more. Although his strong-willed, dominating nature and initial deceptiveness often caused her feelings for him to be confused and ambivalent, she would make him fall in love with her. The thought that she might fail was so devastating that she simply refused to consider it.

Chapter Seven

As she sipped her coffee the next morning, Jenny found herself aching to question the always approachable Dr. Hermann about Joanna Templeton. But she didn't dare do so until Marian Hermann, following her usual practice, went back to their bedroom to finish dressing. Then, with just the proper amount of concern in her voice, Jenny told Dr. Hermann about Kitty's outburst of the previous evening. "I don't want to interfere, but I think if I understood the situation I might be able to talk to Kitty about it."

He was not deceived; he burst out laughing. "My dear Jenny, how very wise of you. And how very transparent!"

Jenny felt like kicking herself. She should have known the man was far too perceptive to be fooled by her clumsy attempt at subtlety. Her cheeks red with embarrassment, she admitted, "You're right. I wanted to know about Joanna, because—because—"

"Exactly so," Dr. Hermann interrupted in a mild voice. "But I must caution you not to lose your heart to Nicholas. My stepson is no angel when it comes to women. Marian and I never interfere—my wife says she learned her lesson when she tried to prevent Nicholas from marrying Marcia."

Jenny was searching for the courage to ask him why when he shook his head. "I will never discuss my stepson's first marriage with you. That is his personal affair. But there is no reason not to satisfy your curiosity about Miss Templeton. Her father, as you may know, is the senior senator from Arizona. He and Marian's first husband were in school together, and Nicholas has known Joanna since both were children. Last year she left her husband and also her young son; they live in Seattle. She is in the process of divorcing him and has resumed her maiden name. She works in her father's Phoenix office and keeps house for him as well." He smiled charmingly at Jenny. "Does that tell you what you wish to know?"

"You've met her?" What Jenny really meant was, Is she pretty?

"Ah, how foolish of me. What you most wish to know is what Miss Templeton looks like."

Jenny blushed all over again. Oscar Hermann was far too shrewd!

"Fairly tall, perhaps 5′8″, very slender, pale blond hair for which I expect she can thank her hairdresser." He chuckled at the thought of it. "She's about thirty years old, and quite beautiful. And, like all of my stepson's 'friends,' sophisticated and experienced."

"Unlike me." Jenny knew that Oscar Hermann was thinking the words, even though he didn't say them.

"Yes, Jenny. Unlike you. Marian is concerned and

quite rightly so. You are more than attractive, my dear. You are eye-catching. Marian and I have noticed the way Nicholas looks at you. It worries us."

Jenny sought to reassure him. "My father—," she began.

"Precisely. Nicholas would not betray your father's trust. But like all of us, he is quite human. Don't tempt the fates, Jenny."

Jenny nodded. Dr. Hermann sighed, looking with distaste at the cup of cold coffee in front of him. "I'll get you a refill," she offered, picking up the cup and taking it over to the coffeepot. She smiled impishly. "It's the least I can do!"

A few minutes later, Jenny answered the door to find Nick standing alongside Kitty. He frowned suspiciously at her cheerful, "Good morning. Can I get you a cup of coffee or some breakfast?"

"No. I wanted to tell you to have Kitty ready at 5:30. See that she changes into a dress."

"You already told me that," Kitty put in. "I'll be good, Daddy. I'll talk to Grandpa Joe."

Nick picked up the child to hug and kiss her. "Off to talk to Grandpa. I want a word with Jenny."

Kitty skipped obediently away, and Jenny murmured, "Sounds ominous."

"You're in a good mood this morning." Nick sounded as if he felt in just the opposite.

At one time, Jenny would have retorted, Yes, because I don't have to cook for *you* tonight. Now she merely agreed, "No cooking, no cleaning, no laundry. Why shouldn't I be?"

"Because last night . . ." he started, then changed his mind. "No reason." He walked to the kitchen, exchanged a few words with Oscar, and left the house.

leaving Jenny wondering what he had wanted to talk to her about.

Jenny and Kitty spent a delightful day together. Kitty loved to read aloud, so Jenny sat back and let herself be entertained for a while. When Kitty tired of reading, Jenny took her window shopping. They were unable to resist entering one posh children's shop they discovered. Jenny still had a sizable portion of Nick's two hundred dollars, and she was sure he would have no objection if she helped Kitty select something for her wardrobe.

"How about a dress for tonight? Something really special?" In the back of her mind was the thought that if they could find a dress that Kitty was eager to wear, she would be more enthusiastic about the dinner.

But Kitty was already rummaging through the racks. She eventually selected a yellow and white sundress of a silk-like synthetic fabric; it had a blouson top, short sleeves, and a draw-string neckline, and was so stylish that Jenny could have worn a larger version of it. A pair of white sandals completed the outfit.

Well pleased with the results of their shopping, they sauntered from the store arm-in-arm and walked along the street, passing a beauty salon which Kitty recognized immediately. "That's where Grandma has her hair done," she said.

All week Jenny had itched to take scissors to the child's hair. Her eyebrows had long ago disappeared under her bangs, and her ends were badly split and needed trimming. "If they can take you, do you want to get your hair cut?" Jenny was careful to sound quite indifferent about the matter.

"I *hate* getting my hair cut." Kitty looked as though she were waiting for Jenny to convince her, but Jenny knew enough about little girls and hair not to bother trying. "Okay then. Let's go to a nice air-conditioned restaurant and have some lunch."

"Do you really think I should have it cut?" The girl wasn't moving from the entrance to the salon.

Jenny pretended to study Kitty's hair. "Just a little, I think."

The proprietress greeted Kitty with, "You're Mrs. Hermann's granddaughter! Are you going to let us cut your hair?" She looked at Jenny, silently adding, Please!

All the operators were busy, but the owner insisted on skipping her lunch to take care of Kitty herself. In the end, she talked the child into far more than a trim. Her hair was cut to shoulder length and tapered down from a center part to flip back. "You're very lucky," she told Kitty. "Your hair falls this way beautifully. And if you want to be especially glamorous, you can always use a curling iron, like I did."

Jenny loved the hairstyle, as did Kitty. In fact, she only agreed to go swimming after lunch if Jenny would promise to comb and curl her hair for her later on. This necessitated a quick trip to the Hermanns to pick up Jenny's curling iron and blow dryer; afterward Jenny helped Kitty dress. She had the twin advantages of height and slimness, and with her new dress and hairdo looked several years older than her age.

As she inspected her appearance in the mirror, she said to Jenny, "Now Joanna won't be able to talk to me like I'm a baby, will she?"

"If she does, she'll only sound foolish. Don't pay any attention to it," Jenny advised.

They were listening to music in the living room when

Nick walked in. Kitty immediately stood up and twirled around, eager for his approval. At first he looked stunned, and Jenny was afraid she had made a colossal blunder. But then he let out a low wolf whistle. "Nichole Jennifer Butler, you look terrific. You can talk Grandpa Joe into doubles on dessert tonight, he'll be so smitten."

"Oh, honestly Daddy, that's for kids!" Kitty giggled.

By now Nick's attention was on Jenny. She felt a rush of pleasure at the warmth in his eyes as he thanked her.

"Beauty has a price," she responded lightly. "The dress, the shoes, the haircut—"

"Were worth whatever they cost," Nick finished. "And now I know the answer to the question that's been plaguing me for the last month. Does my daughter have eyebrows?" he asked teasingly. He held out his arm and Kitty took it, her face glowing with excitement.

Jenny accompanied them out the door, and waved good-bye as she climbed into her car and drove away. All the way home, and all through a quiet dinner with the Hermanns, she thought about Nick, who had looked unbearably handsome in his dark suit, laughing and talking with the beautiful Joanna. Although later, lying awake in bed, she pictured the two of them in more intimate circumstances, her dreams turned out to be much more pleasant. The shadowy silver-blond goddess in Nick's arms was replaced by a dark-haired, dark-eyed facsimile of Jenny who permitted her lover nighttime liberties that the morning Jennifer Ross blushed to remember.

Nick and Kitty came by for breakfast the following morning, and once the Hermanns were finished admiring Kitty's hair-cut the conversation turned to the Templetons' dinner party. Among the other guests had been a couple named Lang and their eleven year old son. "He goes to the same school I'm going to, only he'll be a year ahead of me," Kitty chirped. "He was real cute."

So cute, Nick teased her, that she and Christopher had disappeared immediately after dinner, leaving Grandpa Joe to pine in silence for her. "He did not," Kitty said, her tone relegating her father to the ranks of the hopeless. "He was with Mrs. Post and they were holding hands."

Jenny couldn't resist needling Nick, saying to Kitty, "When you're old enough to date, I'll bet your daddy's going to check out all your boyfriends. He'll probably give them the third degree before he even lets them into the house."

"You're darn right," Nick agreed. "I have to keep her away from guys like me." He was laughing as he spoke, but then his eye caught Jenny's and the smile turned into a frown. "Kitty and I are going to Sedona for the weekend," he announced. "We'll be back Sunday night."

Jenny asked where Sedona was, and Dr. Hermann replied that it was a small, arty town in the northern part of the state. "It's in the midst of an area that I find the most beautiful in Arizona. Nicholas owns a house there. It's much cooler than Phoenix; in fact, Marian and I once left Scottsdale in 100° heat and had to drive through a snowstorm north of Flagstaff."

"I could do with a little snow right now," Jenny replied.

"Maybe it will snow when we go to the Grand

Canyon." Kitty turned to her father. "I want Jenny to come with us. Please?"

"We'll see." The words were equivocal, but the tone said no. To Jenny's relief, Kitty didn't argue.

Nick and Kitty left for Sedona directly from the Hermanns. With a free weekend ahead of her, Jenny's first thought was to follow up Mary's lead about a workshop where she might be able to work on her jewelry. Glancing at the address Mary had written down, Jenny recognized the name of the street as one in the same general area where she and Kitty had shopped the day before. She selected several samples of her work to take with her: a watchband, necklace, a concha belt, earrings. They were among her favorites, pieces she liked too much to sell.

The proprietors, Mr. and Mrs. Barber, were coolly polite when Jenny told them why she had come. Then she pulled out her samples, inviting them to study the work while she browsed around the store. It was the kind of shop where everything seemed vaguely disorganized, giving the place an artistic feel. The jewelry in the glass cases was moderately priced, standard fare. A sign on the wall invited, "Please ask to see our antiques and fine jewelry." Jenny assumed that unusual or valuable items were kept in a safe.

Rugs were suspended from racks, ready to be flipped through; most of them were of recent vintage and good quality. There were also baskets, pottery, paintings and a selection of Indian-made garments and artifacts.

When Jenny returned to the Barbers, she could see that they were impressed by her work. But they looked doubtful. "It's very good, dear. But there's so much of this type of thing around. People like to know they're getting something special," Mrs. Barber said gently, excusing herself to attend to some customers.

Jenny pulled out her wallet with its pictures of her grandmother and great-grandfather. Before she could even say his Indian name, which translated into "Maker of Dancing Silver," Mr. Barber was bending down to open the safe, which Jenny saw was hidden by a Navajo rug just below the level of the counter. He pulled out a squash blossom necklace, wrought entirely in silver except for a square piece of turquoise centered beneath the top of the crescent-shaped naja, or pendant, at the bottom. "Your great-grandfather's. We acquired it last year." He handed it to Jenny to examine.

"It's incredible the work he did, considering that in those days they had to work with silver coins, charcoal and bellows." She fingered the necklace lovingly. "I inherited several of his pieces from my grandmother."

"I'll be honest with you, Jenny. A lot of this business is hype. The fact that you're part Indian will help sell your work. The fact that your great-grandfather was one of the great Indian artists of his time is going to help even more."

Jenny nodded. Naturally, she would have preferred that her work sell purely on its merits. She knew it was as good as at least half of what the store carried, and soon it would be even better. But if an accident of ancestry gave her a leg up, she wasn't about to complain.

Mr. Barber went on, "It's only fair to tell you that you probably won't make a living on what we can sell for you. If you have a job, don't quit. If you don't, get one."

It was not Jenny's usual practice to drop names, but

somehow she couldn't resist. "I'm lucky," she said ingenuously. "I have lots of free time. I'm a mother's helper and housekeeper for a couple named Oscar and Marian Hermann. I take care of their granddaughter. Her father is—"

"Nick Butler of AMT," Mr. Barber finished. "You should have told us that when you walked in."

Jenny found it intimidating that Nick was so well-known and important in this city. "I should have?" she echoed. "Why?"

Mr. Barber smiled. "Because he's a friend as well as our landlord. AMT owns a lot of real estate in this area, including half our block."

Jenny was glad that she hadn't told them about Nick right away and that her ancestry, rather than his connections, had provided the extra pull needed to win the Barbers over. Before she left, she learned that their workshop was located in a lower rent area of Scottsdale, and that weekends and afternoons were the best time to work there. Classes in jewelry making were held several weekday mornings and evenings, and during those times expert craftsmen would be available to provide assistance should Jenny need it.

Jenny wanted very much to repay the Hermanns for their indulgence and kindness, and she decided that her first project would be gifts for their wedding anniversary. She had no difficulty in deciding on a present for Marian: she would fashion a silver bead choker. Oscar was a more challenging proposition. He wore no jewelry other than a plain gold wedding band. Even his watchband was leather, not the inlaid silver so popular in the southwest.

Finally Jenny settled on a silver bookmark inlaid with

turquoise. In most of her jewelry, Jenny emphasized the silver rather than the stonework, and the design of the bookmark would be a departure for her. She planned to ask one of the instructors at the Barbers' school for help.

She spent a good part of the weekend and much of her free time over the next week at the shop. In order to make beads for the necklace, she cut round discs from lightweight silver sheeting. Using a punch and die set, each disc was embossed with the delicate flowered design Jenny had selected, so that the disc became a beautifully decorated little dome. Jenny then filed the edges of each dome smooth, punched a center hole in the top for stringing, and used an acetylene torch to solder pairs of domes together to make the beads. Each bead was cleaned in an acid solution, filed and polished. Next, Jenny made tiny beads of silver wire to string between the larger hollow beads in order to give the necklace a more fragile look. Finally, the beads were strung and a hook and eyelet added at the ends.

After discussing the bookmark project with several of the school's instructors, Jenny decided to incorporate Hopi-style overlay work into the design. She cut two dagger-like patterns from medium-weight silver sheeting. On the heavier piece, she drew an abstract design of her own creation, using as inspiration a navajo rug motif. Each segment of this design was cut out using a jeweler's saw, the silver cleaned, and the solid piece soldered underneath. Several segments of the design had been carefully measured and cut to exactly accommodate flat pieces of turquoise Jenny had previously cut and polished, a technique called channel work. The turquoise was set using a commercial glue, the silver polished and the cut-out segments of the design textured and darkened with an antiquing fluid. Both Jenny and the instructor who had helped her were well pleased with the results.

Nick and Kitty had returned Sunday night, as scheduled, but Jenny saw little of her charge during the week. The Hermanns' next-door neighbors were entertaining their grandson and granddaughter, ages eleven and nine, and Kitty was overjoyed at the prospect of having companions her own age. Most days the neighbors planned sight-seeing jaunts for the morning and swimming in their own pool for the afternoon. They insisted on including Kitty, so that Jenny found herself with some much-needed free time.

With Kitty out of earshot, Jenny was able to attend to the arrangements for the Hermanns' anniversary party in addition to working on her gifts. She finished the necklace and bookmark, sneaking them back into the house and burying them underneath some clothing in her top drawer. The Hermanns made polite inquiries as to how she was spending her time, and seemed satisfied with her vague answers about reading or working in the shop.

She cooked dinner for Nick and Kitty on Monday, Tuesday and Wednesday nights, and was both hurt and amused at how assiduously Nick avoided being alone with her. Rather than risk the solitude of the living room or bedroom, he would retreat to the den to watch television with Kitty while Jenny prepared dinner. He was polite but impersonal during these meals, addressing most of his comments to Kitty and limiting his exchanges with Jenny to two or three sentences. The warmer and more agreeable she was, the more annoyed he seemed. By the time Jenny left on Wednesday, the atmosphere had become positively arctic.

Given Nick's increasing iciness, Jenny was more than a little bewildered when he strolled into the Barbers' workshop at noon on Thursday. She noticed him only seconds before he spotted her at her workbench. Several brisk strides brought him to her side.

"I'm taking you out to lunch," he informed her in his usual high-handed manner.

It was difficult for Jenny to prevent herself from uttering a sarcastic question as to why she was being thus honored, but she managed it. "That's nice," she answered lightly. "It will be a change from the local burger stand."

She straightened up her tools and walked out with Nick, who showed no inclination to explain the reason for his invitation. After they were seated in his little sports car, he never seemed to drive the Rolls, Jenny's curiosity won out over her determination to act just as coolly as Nick always seemed to.

"Is there something special you wanted to talk about?" she asked.

"Things between us are too tense. Kitty's starting to notice. I thought if we got to know each other better, so we had more to talk about, it might help to defuse the situation."

Jenny welcomed any opportunity to spend time alone with Nick, even if she suspected that an intimate lunch would only intensify the attraction on her side. Just sitting next to him in the small sports car was enough to make her whole body tingle.

He took her to one of Scottsdale's most elegant restaurants. At first Jenny was self-conscious about her jeans and brightly-colored print blouse, but a glance around the room told her that others were just as casually attired.

"Only one ground rule," Nick said as they were seated. "Forget you work for me. If we talk about Kitty or your job, we'll wind up arguing, so we won't talk about them. Agreed?"

It was probably a sensible approach, Jenny admitted to herself as she nodded at Nick. "So tell me about your company, and what you hope to accomplish in the future," she said.

Nick responded with a brief history of AMT's growth from a small, intrastate trucking company to a business employing thousands of people in six different states. His enthusiasm was a revelation to Jenny, who had come to know only his cynical, arrogant side. She was particularly impressed by his plans for the next four years, and by the strong sense of responsibility he felt toward his employees.

Although Jenny spoke briefly about her jewelry making, she was much more interested in learning about Nick than in talking about herself. He was surprisingly responsive to her questions, even though he seemed to be increasingly tense as lunch progressed.

Jenny's admiration of him was heightened by the two glasses of wine she consumed. As they sipped their coffee, she rested her elbows on the table, leaning forward to gaze raptly into Nick's eyes as he spoke. She almost dropped her cup when he barked out, "Jenny, if you keep looking at me that way, you know where we're going to wind up—so cut it out!"

His icy comment destroyed the amicable mood between them. The atmosphere became charged with all the old sexual tension, so that Jenny was relieved when it was time to go. After her halting attempts to continue the conversation were met by monosyllabic rebuffs, she lapsed into silence. She couldn't wait to get out of the car when they reached the workshop, and groaned inwardly when the handle of the door refused to budge.

"Now the rotten thing starts sticking again!" Nick muttered, reaching over to fiddle with it. Jenny leaned back against the seat, trying to ignore the way Nick's arm was pressed against her breasts. His head was practically touching her own, and all she could think of was what would happen if he turned his neck even a fraction of an inch.

After he succeeded in opening the door, there were four or five long seconds when he and Jenny stared straight into each other's eyes, their faces only inches apart. Jenny knew she should leave, but somehow couldn't; the desire she saw on Nick's face held her spellbound.

But his voice held only ice as he snapped, "Out of the car, Jenny. On second thought, this was a lousy idea!"

She scrambled out to the sidewalk, jumping at the sound of the door being slammed after her. Resentment mingled with embarrassment. Nick seemed to blame her for the fact that he found her desirable. At the same time, whenever she allowed her own growing feelings for him to show, he withdrew into an icy shell.

Her aggravation grew when he phoned the shop later that afternoon to curtly inform her that he would be working until 8:30 and would pick Kitty up at the Hermanns'. He was no more polite when he appeared at his mother's later that evening. Jenny watched with mounting fury as he greeted Oscar, Marian and Kitty with the usual smiling affection, but barely even acknowledged her presence.

As he was leaving, his eyes slid coldly over her body, and in a voice that matched the temperature of his gaze, he told her, "You can cook dinner tomorrow night, Jenny."

Jenny swallowed the explosive retort she wanted to make and merely nodded curtly at him. Then she turned away, her eyes inexplicably full of tears.

On Friday evening, Jenny decided that she would have to see Nick alone to discuss arrangements for the anniversary party. She invited Kitty's new friends for dinner, suggesting that they go into Kitty's room to listen to music. They chose a rock album so ear-splitting that Nick was forced to take refuge in the living room. Jenny couldn't help but gloat over the success of her stratagem.

Nick had not even deigned to wish her a good evening, and suddenly Jenny was gripped by a mischievous urge to exact retribution for his continuing beastly behavior toward her. She sashayed into the living room and sat down on the couch, her thigh touching his. She was wearing only her bikini and, over it, a semi-transparent, net shirt. "I have to talk to you," she whispered urgently.

Nick immediately moved to a chair, frowning moodily at her impish grin. "Don't play games with me," he said irritably. "What is it?"

"We have to talk about the anniversary party. Alone. Unless you want me to call in Kitty, so she can broadcast it to your mother and stepfather?" The glint

in her dark eyes mocked him, and it was clear from the
ice in his own blue eyes and the whiteness around his
mouth that he was having difficulty remaining stoic in
the face of her needling.

He folded his arms across his chest and responded to
the progress report she gave him with curt nods of
approval and even curter supplementary instructions.
Jenny couldn't help but find it funny, and when he had
delivered the final order—"I'm supposedly taking
everyone out to dinner Saturday night, even you Miss
Ross. Have them here at 6:30"—her self-control
crumbled. She leaned her head against the back of the
couch and laughed. She expected Nick to stalk out of
the room, but he didn't. He waited until she had
succeeded in containing her outburst, then remarked,
"So you think it's funny?"

"Well it is!" Jenny insisted. "It was bad enough
before we had lunch, but since yesterday you've been
treating me like someone who robs little old ladies of
their handbags. It's not my fault if you—"

"I'm going out tomorrow night. I want you here
to baby-sit. At six." The orders were barked out in
drill sergeant fashion, prompting Jenny to bolt upright, stand at attention, and deliver a smart salute.
"Yes, *sir!*" she giggled, ignoring Nick's tight-lipped
expression. "Permission to serve dinner, general!"
she added.

Only then did he march out of the room, returning a
few minutes later with the three children in tow and
looking no less angry than when he left.

The next evening, Jenny arrived at six o'clock, as
instructed. Nick's mood hadn't improved overnight.
He handed Jenny a piece of paper listing two names

and phone numbers, the second that of the Templetons. Jenny felt a surge of jealousy because he would be with Joanna.

"I'll be late," he told her. "Go to sleep if you want to." He slammed the door on his way out.

After dinner she and Kitty swam for several hours, played checkers and watched television. Kitty went to bed at ten, while Jenny stayed up to read. By one o'clock she was having difficulty keeping her eyes open.

She lay down on the couch, wondering how much longer Nick was going to be out with Joanna, and soon fell asleep, only to be awakened by a heavy hand on her arm.

"Come on, Jenny. Up and out." The voice was Nick's, the tone as grim as any she had ever heard from him.

Her eyes fluttered open, then closed against the glare of the light. She had been dreaming about Nick—again, and she had no desire to trade her fantasy for cold reality. "I'm so sleepy," she mumbled. "Can't I just stay here?"

A silky female voice brought her fully awake. "Three's a crowd, darling. I think you'd better go home."

The woman standing in the doorway was obviously Joanna Templeton. With her spike heels and pale blond hair combed into a sensuously disarrayed knot atop her head, she was nearly as tall as Nick. Her clinging silver dress was slashed to the waist in front, and Jenny thought uncharitably that the woman certainly didn't like to leave anything to the imagination.

Nick walked back over to Joanna, draping his arm over her shoulder in a casually possessive gesture.

Jenny brushed her own tangled hair from her eyes and rolled off the bed, feeling very much at a disadvantage in her crumpled jeans and shirt.

"Joanna Templeton, Jenny Ross," Nick said, nodding at each of them in turn.

"So you're the little girl Kitty was babbling on about," Joanna said, her mirthless laugh dismissing Jenny as of no importance.

"She had a lot to say about you, too." Jenny paused for maximum effect. "None of it good." She lifted her chin and, picking up her purse, prepared to leave.

As Jenny moved toward them, Nick deliberately turned his back to her and lowered his head to give Joanna a lingering kiss. Jenny had no choice but to wait until they were finished, but when Nick's head lifted, signaling the end of the kiss, he made no move to turn around. "Good-night, Miss Ross." His tone was impersonal; his attention was wholly on Joanna.

Her head down, Jenny slipped past the two of them and left the house. She felt sick to her stomach. For a few minutes she simply sat in her car, digging the nails of one hand into the palm of the other in a futile attempt not to cry.

Two cars sat facing the garage: Nick's Rolls—so he *did* drive it, Jenny thought—and a white Mercedes which Jenny assumed belonged to Joanna. Seeing the cars side by side made her think of Nick and Joanna together, and she hastily started her engine and drove down the driveway. If she hadn't been crying, the sight of the Mercedes would have made her laugh. Trust Nick to tell his ladylove to bring her own car. When he was finished making love to her, he would send her on her way. He couldn't be bothered to drive her home.

Jenny started to head down the mountain, then

changed her mind and made a U-turn to reverse directions. It was very late and the Hermanns would probably be asleep, but on the slim chance that they weren't, she could hardly show up with her face streaked with tears and her eyes puffy from crying. She followed the road as it twisted up the mountain and parked at the dead end. Then she got out and stood in the still-warm nighttime air, looking down to the flatlands below. Then she tipped her head back to gaze at the stars, picking out the constellations and feeling very insignificant.

She tried to tell herself that Nick was in no hurry to marry Joanna Templeton or anyone else. She had known he was very far from a saint; it was only having it demonstrated so graphically that tore her apart. When she pictured Nick making love to Joanna, she felt an acid, wrenching jealousy. How could she possibly compete with this experienced, glamorous creature who had known him since childhood? Jenny was sure that only Kitty's insecurity stood in the way of Nick's remarriage.

And the thought of Nick Butler belonging to someone else was agonizing to Jenny, because she knew she was in love with him and had been almost from the beginning, from their first dinner together in Indio. She finally understood that and admitted it to herself. She was devoted to Kitty and would feel impossibly guilty over leaving her, so she must somehow continue to work for Nick without letting him discover her real feelings. A numbing depression set in.

Chapter Eight

By the end of the following week, Jenny's depression had deepened and her self-confidence was in shreds. Nick had called midmorning on Sunday to say he needed to spend the rest of the day in the office and would drop Kitty off shortly. The Hermanns' neighbors had an afternoon wedding to attend and Jenny had already agreed to watch their grandchildren; Kitty happily joined them in their pool.

When Nick returned after dinner that evening, the children were in Kitty's room constructing a futuristic city out of blocks and Jenny was in her own room, making some sketches for a concha belt she planned to make as Kitty's birthday present.

He walked in without knocking, closing the door behind him. "You were rude to Joanna last night. Try it again and I'll fire you."

Jenny, astonished by the harshness of this delayed

attack, simply stared at him with vulnerable brown eyes. His stance was classically aggressive—feet slightly apart, hands on his hips, expression condemning. He looked so angry that she thought in dismay that he must love Joanna very much to be so protective of her.

Still, Jenny's rudeness wasn't totally unjustified and she felt she had the right to explain her viewpoint. "I'm sorry you see it that way. I thought Joanna was very sarcastic to me, and—"

"You're an employee. She's a friend," Nick interrupted cuttingly. "I don't care what Joanna or anyone else says to you. Keep the snide retorts to yourself."

Jenny's stomach churned in rebellion and pain. Part of her wanted to pull her suitcase out from under the bed and start packing, but the rest of her couldn't bear the thought of never seeing Nick again. Once she would have exploded, which was what he seemed to expect. Now she was so in love with him that she quickly backed down.

She stood up and walked over to him, desperately aware of the ice in his eyes. "I'm sorry I offended Joanna, Nick. I'll apologize when I see her next Saturday," she said softly.

At least Jenny had the satisfaction of knowing that he was absolutely astonished by her verbal retreat. He quickly recovered, however, and Jenny was afraid he would subject her to one of his curt nods and stalk out of the room. She couldn't bear to have him so angry with her.

She touched his sleeve and said hesitantly, "May I show you something?" Nick stared pointedly at her hand and Jenny, her face hot with embarrassment, removed it.

"Do I have a choice?" He folded his arms in front of his chest and tapped his foot a few times to underscore his impatience.

Jenny walked over to the dresser and unwrapped the necklace and bookmark she had made for the Hermanns. She was certain Nick would be pleased. "For your mother and stepfather. Do you like them?"

Jenny held them out, but Nick declined to take them. His glance was perfunctory. "Not bad." He turned on his heel, opened the door and walked out of the room.

Jenny softly closed the door and leaned against it, looking at the necklace and bookmark. They were a lot more than "not bad." They were beautiful. Would it have been so difficult for Nick to praise her? His deliberately cold appraisal hurt her even more than his earlier stinging rebuke. Fighting back tears, she gently rewrapped the items in tissue paper and slipped them back in her drawer.

The rest of the week had been a cold war. Nick was in Los Angeles Monday and Tuesday nights, returning Wednesday morning to accept his mother's invitation to dinner. Jenny had received a phone call earlier in the day from a woman who identified herself as Mr. Butler's secretary, asking if arrangements for the party on Saturday were complete. She tried to ignore the pain that the impersonal inquiry inflicted on her. Nick was obviously determined to avoid her completely, even on the phone.

Given the tension between them, dinner was certain to turn into a disaster. Jenny knew she would end up either screaming or crying, and fabricated a fictitious dinner date to escape the house. She decided to spend the evening working. After stopping at a burger stand for dinner, she drove to the shop. Mr. Barber had been impressed with the necklace Jenny had made for Mrs. Hermann, and had asked her to provide two or three such chokers to sell in the store. She worked on the commission until past 10:30.

She drew up to the Hermanns' and noted with anxiety that Nick's car was still in the driveway. It was so late—why hadn't he left yet? She planned a rapid good-night and hasty retreat to her room, but before she could escape, Nick demanded, "Why are you so late?"

"We were talking—about jewelry making," Jenny improvised.

"Who were you with?"

It was really none of his business, but Jenny knew that if she said so, Nick would only demand an answer. Even the Hermanns looked silently at Jenny, waiting for her reply.

Jenny had become friendly with a young Navajo silversmith, named Jim Maloma, whose bold, original designs had won him numerous prizes throughout the southwest. He seemed a likely prospect for her would-be dinner partner. "His name is Jim Maloma," she said coolly, "and he's—"

"I know who he is." Nick flexed his arm to reveal a gold watchband inlaid with spiderweb turquoise. "I also know his wife."

Jenny could have groaned with despair. Hadn't she admired the exquisite silver and coral wedding ring Jim wore? Why hadn't she picked someone more obscure?

"We spent the evening *talking*," she murmured defensively. "We're just friends."

"Which is how you'll stay. Leave him alone." Jenny was ready to insist that she would see whomever she chose when the absurdity of the situation hit her. She was ready to protest an order by Nick that she stop seeing a man she had never dated in the first place. In addition to all her other sins, Nick was now condemning her as some sort of homewrecker. She managed a haughty, "If you say so, Mr. Butler," before fleeing to her room.

She dawdled over dressing the next morning, waiting until the Hermanns left the house before emerging for breakfast. Kitty had arrived earlier and was perched on Jenny's bed, watching her pin up her hair. She informed Jenny that her father would be picking her up sometime after dinner; he had an evening meeting to attend.

Jenny expected him to avoid her on Friday as well, but Kitty passed on the message that she was to prepare dinner. As usual, the child had greeted her father with a hug when he got home and went off to watch TV. Jenny was slicing raw vegetables for a salad, her fingers becoming clumsy with tension as soon as Nick walked in the house.

"I want to talk to you about tomorrow night."

The voice came from somewhere behind her left shoulder, and carried the usual impatient overtones. Jenny didn't look up—she didn't want Nick to see the nervousness and hurt in her eyes. She simply answered, "Yes?"

Nick grasped her arm and swung her around so forcefully that she dropped her knife on the floor, missing her bare foot by less than an inch. "Why the devil don't you wear shoes?" he snarled. "And look at me when I speak to you!"

Jenny took a deep breath. She felt that if she tried to

speak, she would end up sobbing. Her "Sorry" was little more than a whisper.

If Nick noticed her bereft expression, it had no effect on him. "I'm taking Kitty out for the day tomorrow," he informed Jenny. "The caterers will be here at two to set up. I want you here to help them. We'll be back at five."

Jenny nodded her assent and turned back to work. As she tore up the lettuce for the salad a single tear slipped out. She sniffed and impatiently brushed it away, relieved that Nick had left the room and hadn't seen it.

The following afternoon, Jenny pulled up to the house to find two large catering trucks in the driveway. Several people stood by the door, including a burly overall-clad man who was ringing the bell. Jenny hurried over and introduced herself.

The caterers went about their job with impressive efficiency. They supplied everything, from bone-colored, gold-rimmed plates to flatwear, from linens to extra tables and chairs, from glassware to a smorgasbord of beautifully arranged food. Most of the food remained on metal carts in a refrigerated truck, which they pulled into the garage to sit next to Nick's sports car.

A few hours later a petite woman arrived with the flowers—several airy arrangements done in silver bowls and two white orchid corsages. Jenny realized that one of them was for Mrs. Hermann, and wondered dejectedly if the other was for Joanna Templeton.

A truck from the liquor store pulled up next; cases of liquor, beer, mixers and champagne found their way to the bar, to be stored on the floor or in the stainless steel refrigerator. At one point, ten different people were working in the house and yard, the net impression one of chaos. Jenny calmly supervised all of them.

By the time Nick returned at 5:30, there was no sign of the previous whirlwind of activity. Only three women from the caterer's remained, and the house and yard looked beautiful. Seven people piled out of the Rolls: Nick, Kitty and five others Jenny recognized from the picture in the Hermanns' living room as Oscar Hermann's daughter and her family.

"Sorry we're late," Nick apologized as he walked in. "The plane just came in. This is Oscar's family: Dr. Jerry Franklin, Oscar's daughter Mary, and their children Ted, Steve and Kathy. Jenny Ross, who takes care of Kitty."

Jenny smiled her hellos. She was tense in Nick's presence and was about to cover up the feeling with small talk when he put his hands on her shoulders and turned her around to face the door. "Get moving. You have an hour to change and get back here with my parents." His tone was brusque.

It was a deadline Jenny couldn't meet. The Hermanns waited patiently while she put the finishing touches on her makeup. It had taken longer than she expected to do her hair, which was coiled on top of her head, emphasizing her slender neck. She wore the clinging, strapless black silk gown Nick had once admired, admitting to herself that she had chosen it mostly for that reason, but also because the stark style suited her jewelry. Around her neck was an Indian-made squash blossom necklace of gold inlaid with green Persian turquoise, the most exquisite and expensive piece of jewelry she owned. Matching earrings and bracelet completed a picture Jenny hoped would dazzle Nick Butler. She tried not to remember that she was probably wasting her time. It hurt too badly to believe that Joanna Templeton meant everything to Nick and Jennifer Ross meant nothing.

At least Oscar's gallantry was dependable, and it lifted Jenny's spirits. "You look stunning, my dear," he complimented. "But all this for a simple dinner?"

Jenny muttered something about being in the mood to dress up. Marian Hermann, she noted, was wearing a floating, floor-length creation of silk chiffon, and seemed to be dripping with diamonds.

"Ah yes," Oscar agreed. "As was my wife. Don't forget your bathing suit, Jenny. Nicholas's parties are usually rather wild—they have a way of winding up with half the guests in the pool."

Jenny was about to attempt her best impersonation of utter bewilderment when Oscar's amused expression told her not to bother. "Are you going to pretend to be surprised?" she asked with a smile.

"Of course." The simultaneous answer came from both the Hermanns.

Jenny stuffed her suit into her purse, along with her gifts for the Hermanns, and rejoined them in the hall. On the way to Nick's, Marian told her that it was impossible for them not to know about the surprise party. Too many of their friends had avoided mention of any plans for celebrating their anniversary, and when Marian had devilishly suggested that several of their closest friends come over for dinner, all had been mysteriously busy and asked for rainchecks.

The guests' cars were parked in a neighbor's driveway but had spilled out onto the main road. Oscar drove through the open gate and pulled up by his stepson's front door, then led everyone up to the entrance and gave a few quick knocks. The door was opened by Kitty, who looked enchanting in pink and white lace, and who led the chorus of "Surprise!" and "Happy Anniversary!"

The Hermanns' imitation of unadulterated astonishment was worthy of an award. Jenny knew that both of them were genuinely surprised by the presence of Mary Franklin and her family, and when she noticed the white orchid on Mary's wrist she shuddered with relief. Thank goodness the corsage hadn't been for Joanna! The Hermanns were soon lost in the sea of people waiting to offer congratulations and kisses, and when Jenny next saw Mrs. Hermann she had her own white orchid pinned in her hair.

She had promised Nick that she would apologize to Joanna, and by the time she came across the slender blonde goddess two margaritas made the thought of it easier to bear. Joanna was clad in a theatrical, dazzling outfit consisting of full-cut, swirling gold pants, a strapless jet black top adorned with tiny sequins, and a long-sleeved jacket that matched her pants. Jenny steeled herself to approach the woman, who was surrounded by a group of admiring men.

She joined them with the practiced ease she had acquired during years of attending her grandmother's parties, exchanging friendly hellos with Joanna's covey of admirers. "I wanted to apologize for the other night," she said to the sophisticated blonde. "I was very rude and I'm sorry."

Joanna seemed to look right through her. "I'm sorry," she said vaguely, "I don't remember. . . ." Her confusion was ample explanation, and with a hastily repressed giggle Jenny realized that Joanna didn't recognize her.

"Jenny Ross. Kitty's baby-sitter," she explained. Joanna looked stunned, her eyes on the necklace around Jenny's throat.

A gray-haired man dressed in a casual suit and cowboy boots took up the slack in the conversation. "I'm glad to know you, Jenny," he said, patting her shoulder proprietorially. "I'm Joe Templeton, Joanna's father. Can't say I always agree with your father's politics, but he sure produced a beautiful little girl."

"Thank you. It's nice to meet you too, Senator. Maybe I'll persuade my father to run for the Senate, just to plague you," she teased.

The senator took a healthy swallow of his drink and laughed uproariously at this gentle jest. "Heaven help us! We'd better keep him in California. I'll even contribute to his next campaign!"

"You seem to know something I don't, Daddy," Joanna inserted with a stiff smile. "Who is Jenny's father?"

"Emerson Ross, the Assembly Speaker over in California. Trust Nick to make all the right connections." He patted Jenny's shoulder again. "And the little lady's grandfather is one of the smartest city lawyers in the west."

Joanna's smile was as frigid as the frozen daiquiri in her hand. She covered up her reaction to this piece of news by sipping the drink and slipped away at the first opportunity. Jenny stayed on to chat with the senator and his friends. She thought smugly that Joanna Templeton had marked her down as a little nobody, and for the first time in her life was actually pleased that her father and grandfather were both well-known and influential.

For the next few hours she nibbled on samples of the delicious food and met so many people that she gave up trying to remember their names. At one point she tried to count the guests, and came up with a figure exceeding one hundred and fifty people. They were spread out through the house, bar and backyard. Every now and then she noticed Nick in this throng, usually with Joanna on his arm. Jenny relied on an additional margarita to soothe the pain this caused her.

It was not until after the champagne toast that the party began to heat up. Nick had gathered everyone outside on the floodlit patio while the caterers and bartenders passed out glasses of champagne. The circular, glass-topped table was stacked with gifts, among them those from Jenny.

The band struck up "Happy Anniversary to You" and the assembled guests sang two raucous choruses. Fortunately, Jenny thought, Nick had invited all of his neighbors. Otherwise they would surely be complaining to the police about the noise.

Suddenly the floodlights were cut off and a candle-lit, four-tiered cake wheeled out. By now it was dark and the dramatic appearance of the cake occasioned great applause and a few whistles. The band swung into "The Anniversary Waltz," Oscar took Marian in his arms, and everyone cheered and clapped.

Afterward, the lights were turned back on and the Hermanns opened their presents. The band continued to play and many of the guests began to dance. Oscar and Marian were greatly touched by Jenny's necklace and bookmark, the more so because they apparently hadn't expected anything from her.

As always, Jenny needed no excuse to join in the dancing. The first slow number found Joanna in Nick's arms, held in a manner that Jenny told herself was disgustingly intimate. She ignored the little voice that told her that she had once danced just as intimately with him herself.

Most of the music was either throbbing rock, or sensuous, pulsing Latin rhythms. Jenny's dancing became progressively more uninhibited as the evening wore on, and although she was aware that she had drunk too much champagne and too many margaritas, she told herself that she was no different from most of the other guests.

She was enveloped in such a lovely haze that she never noticed how angry Nick looked every time he happened to glance her way. By 11:30, as Mrs. Hermann had predicted, people began to abandon dancing in favor of swimming. They would disappear into the cabanas and emerge in their suits to jump or dive into the brightly lit pool. There was a good deal of horseplay and Jenny noticed several husky young men appear, apparently out of nowhere, to monitor the activities.

Suddenly Jenny felt like swimming, but first she wanted to dance with Nick. She had waited all night for him to ask her and was hurt and angry that he had made no move to do so. He might have asked her at least for appearance's sake, she thought. The band began to play a red-hot version of a sixties hit, and Jenny simply pulled him away from Joanna as they stood on the sidelines.

Jenny knew perfectly well that he would have refused to dance except for the implicit pressure from his friends, who began to cheer wildly the moment she dragged him away from Joanna. She could tell he was angry, but assumed it was only because she had railroaded him into a dance he would rather have skipped.

When the number ended, Jenny's attention was again caught by the frolicking and laughter from the pool. She handed her jewelry to one of Nick's stolid lifeguards, who was sitting with a stack of manila envelopes filled with diamonds, emeralds and sapphires. A minute later she had fetched her suit from the house and was half-walking, half-dancing to the rear cabana.

Carefully locking the door, she slithered out of her black gown. The cabana compartment was spacious, about six feet by five. Along one wall was a cushioned bench with several throw pillows tossed on it; a second wall was covered by a floor to ceiling mirror and a closet ran the length of the third.

Jenny hung the dress alongside the others in the closet and inspected her image in the mirror. She was pleased by what she saw, even though her reflection was showing an alarming tendency to waver. She pulled on her bikini and considered her hair. It would be better to take it down, she thought. She was in the process of pulling out the pins when the door opened.

Chapter Nine

Nick Butler, clad in his maroon bathing suit, strolled in as though he owned the place, which of course he did, Jenny thought with a giggle. In a more sober moment she would have recognized the expression on his face for what it was—pure anger—but she was reckless tonight and in no mood to let anything or anyone ruin her evening.

"Hi!" she said cheerfully. "Another one of your master keys, Nick?"

"That's right. Children have been known to lock themselves in." His tone made it quite clear just who he considered to be a child. Jenny continued to take her hair down, meeting Nick's disapproving stare in the mirror.

"You're making a real spectacle of yourself, do you know that? If one more friend of mine comes up and pokes me in the ribs and makes a cheap crack about falling for the baby-sitter . . ."

The rest of the sentence was bitten off in apparent exasperation as Nick continued to watch Jenny in the mirror. She was running her fingers through her hair to smooth it, her movements unconsciously lazy and erotic. When he persisted in staring at her, she turned around and asked, "Where's your sense of humor? Or is Joanna complaining because you stopped dancing attendance on her?" As soon as the words were out, she regretted them.

Nick's eyes narrowed ominously. "You enjoy the attention, don't you Jenny? That's why you act like you're for sale to the highest bidder." His fingers closed around her upper arms. "Fine. We'll go outside and auction you off."

Nick had begun to half-drag, half-carry her toward the cabana door when Jenny suddenly realized that he was blazingly angry. Why hadn't she noticed that before? In his present mood, he seemed capable of making her the star attraction in a painfully embarrassing sideshow. She began to struggle away from him, leaning back and trying to pull her arms free. "You'll embarrass your parents. Let go of me," she gasped.

He did so, but only to grasp her waist instead. Jenny was afraid he was going to pick her up and sling her over his shoulder like a sack of laundry. She tried to twist out of his firm hold, pushing at his bare chest with her hands. A moment later, she found her feet off the floor and, panic-stricken, begged miserably, "Please, Nick. Don't."

"I'm only giving you what you asked for," he answered, his voice so full of raw dislike that Jenny suddenly and uncontrollably burst into tears.

Nick muttered a few well-chosen obscenities, simultaneously dumping her onto the padded bench. He stood with his back to her, waiting for her to stop crying, every muscle in his body rigid. Only after she succeeded in controlling her sobs did he turn around to acknowledge her presence, and to Jenny's relief his anger and hostility seemed to have disappeared. His tone was dryly amused as he told her, "I wasn't really going to do it, you know. I was going to throw you into the pool."

"Oh." Jenny felt extremely foolish. She should have known Nick would never spoil the Hermanns' party by creating an embarrassing scene.

"And I didn't come here to yell at you," he added in a low, husky voice, "although that's what I told myself ten minutes ago."

Jenny stared up at him, about to ask why he *had* come, and then had no need for explanations. The way Nick's eyes were roaming over her body told her more than words could have. He took a few steps toward the door, locked it and clicked off the light switch. It was pitch black in the little cabana.

She felt him sit down close beside her on the bench, her heart slamming against her ribcage with a violent rapidity that made her dizzy. Nick's hands reached out to find her, came into contact with her shoulders, then slid under her arms to pull her forward. The next thing Jenny knew, Nick was on his back, half-lying and half-sitting on the bench, and she was lying on top of him.

He adjusted a few throw pillows behind him in an effort to make himself comfortable and slid down a little further, his mouth nuzzling Jenny's temple as his hands made short work of removing the top half of her bikini.

Jenny was only half-aware of her fingernails digging

into his arms, her mouth raining fevered kisses on his neck and face. She was overwhelmed by what Nick was doing to her, both with his whole body, which was pressed intimately along the length of hers, and with his hands, which caressed every inch of bare skin. When he dragged her upward to expose her breasts to his tongue and teeth, she trembled with violent pleasure, moaning his name softly.

Then he pushed her roughly down again, seizing her hair and turning her face up to receive his kiss. There were none of the deliberately arousing maneuvers Jenny had come to expect, only the demanding feel of his lips and tongue and teeth, hard and insistent and searching, and the sound of his breathing, heavy and erratic.

Jenny's arms were pinned under Nick's back as she responded with uninhibited passion. But as Nick's hands became more demanding, she suddenly remembered that although he found her physically desirable, he didn't love her. She was insane to permit him to touch her this way, no matter how strong her feelings for him were. She shifted her weight to lessen the intimacy of the embrace, an action that Nick apparently misinterpreted. He pulled his mouth away to mutter, "My back is killing me, too," then struggled to a sitting position, unceremoniously pushing Jenny off his lap.

As he reached over to click on the light, he drawled, "It may be the right time, but it's sure as hell the wrong place." Jenny said nothing. She was confused and much too frightened of rejection to ask him what he planned. Her face was red with embarrassment as she caught Nick's eyes on her naked breasts, and she hastily put her suit top back on.

"I think we need to talk, Jenny."

Jenny's whispered "Yes?" was hoarse and tense.

"I want to make love to you—very much. But I won't get married. I don't want commitments."

A shiver fluttered through Jenny's body and she huddled on the bench, trying not to tremble. "You mean—you want me to live with you," she said, trying to hide her disappointment.

"No!" The syllable exploded angrily. "The last fight I had with Marcia was over the fact that she let Paul move in. I'm no hypocrite."

"I don't understand," Jenny managed.

"Kitty goes to bed at nine or ten o'clock. She's a sound sleeper. We'll have time to be together."

The picture Nick was painting was all too clear, and Jenny was both angry and more deeply hurt than she could ever let him know. What on earth did he think she was?

"I see," she said, nodding slowly. "Jenny makes the dinner, Jenny puts Kitty to bed and then Jenny puts Nick to bed. Charming." She straightened and sat up, stiffly waiting for Nick's reply, hoping desperately that somehow he would deny her view of his proposition, tell her he loved her, claim he needed more time.

He did none of these things. In a cool voice, he stated, "I've never been dishonest about my feelings for you. I could seduce you with empty words and phony promises, but I don't operate that way. I want you and it's obvious you want me. Yes or no?"

Jenny knew she could never handle such a cold-blooded arrangement. When it ended, as it would have to end, her emotions and self-esteem would be in shreds. She simply shook her head and waited for Nick to walk out.

Instead, he took her face in his hands and smiled

down at her. "I had a feeling you'd refuse. But you aren't being logical, Jenny. I care about you. I can make you happy. As long as we're together, I promise there will be no one else. When you change your mind, I'll be waiting." He released her, stood up, and let himself out of the cabana.

Jenny stared at the closed door, her emotions in a tangle. A part of her felt ecstatic that Nick should say he cared for her. She knew that if he were proposing such an arrangement, Joanna Templeton must be much less important than she had assumed. But at the same time, she found his egotistical overconfidence as objectionable as ever and was insulted by his proposition. She wondered what had happened to his pompous promise to her father. Presumably he had decided that it applied only in the case of seduction, not if her acquiescence were freely and previously obtained.

During the rest of the evening, she joined in the water sports taking place in the pool and allowed herself to be claimed for several poolside dances, but her heart wasn't really in it. From time to time she noticed Nick on the patio talking to various guests but he never even looked her way.

The last group of guests left at two o'clock. The family had retired to the den to drink coffee and talk quietly. Jenny helped the caterers clean up and pack. Afterward, she went to the cabana to change into her dress, retrieved the manila envelope with her jewelry, and went inside.

She immediately felt chilled. It was at least ten degrees warmer outside than inside. Nick's suit jacket was slung over the cushioned back of a living room chair; with a yawn, Jenny curled up in the chair and put the jacket over her like a blanket. It smelled of Nick's aftershave lotion, she thought, as she fell into an exhausted sleep.

It was a three-day holiday weekend and since Oscar's family was there it was natural for everyone to spend the remaining two days together. They swam, picnicked and talked, went out for brunch and dinner, took a drive around the city and recuperated from the party. Jenny made no protest about being included. Nick was friendly but distant with her, treating her exactly like any young woman in whom he had no personal interest.

At first she was wary and tense in his presence, half-afraid he would proposition her again and perversely disappointed when he didn't. By the end of the weekend, however, she had relaxed, allowing herself to hope that Nick's caring would eventually turn to love.

Kitty returned to school the following Wednesday, escorted by her protective father. Housework and shopping took up less than half of Jenny's time, and she was able to work on a concha belt for Kitty's birthday present as well as the necklaces commissioned by the Barbers.

Nick took business trips to California and the Pacific Northwest and was gone several nights a week; other evenings he accepted his mother's invitations to dinner. Over the next few weeks, Jenny cooked only a handful of meals for him. About two and a half weeks after the party, he had come into the kitchen as Jenny stir-fried some beef and vegetables, put a hand on her shoulder and said softly, "Changed your mind yet?" She shook her head, whereupon he nibbled her neck and then walked away, leaving her breathless with wanting him.

He gave the impression of a man who knew what he wanted and was willing to wait for it—at least for a while. His manner was relaxed and charming, whether talking with Jenny about her work and his or asking Kitty about school, and he never lost his temper. If desire for Jenny was causing him sleepless nights, he gave no sign of it.

After several weeks of this treatment, Jenny had become somewhat philosophical about Nick's attitude. Although she knew none of the details of his first marriage, she understood that he had been miserably unhappy. Perhaps his subsequent experiences with women like Joanna Templeton had given him a negative impression of the female sex. If he sought a no-strings relationship, perhaps it was only because he felt nothing else would work for him.

Unfortunately, it wouldn't work for her. Nick had no need to pressure her to submit to his wishes: her own feelings for him made it difficult for her to deny him. The love and physical attraction she felt for him intensified as the days passed. Only a strong sense of self-preservation enabled her to continue to reject his proposition. She knew that when the affair ended, she would be utterly devastated.

The night of Kitty's birthday, Marian Hermann invited her son and granddaughter to dinner. Jenny made a chocolate cake for the occasion, and after everyone had finished dinner and feasted on cake and ice cream, Kitty opened her presents.

She adored the concha belt Jenny had crafted and was thrilled that Jenny had thought to make several additional conchas, or shell-shaped pieces of silver, to add to the belt as Kitty grew.

Her grandparents bought her a cassette tape recorder and some tapes; there was a box in the mail from her mother's mother which contained a matching night-gown and robe and some sportswear. Later in the evening, Kitty called her grandmother to thank her, and it was obvious from the conversation that they spoke fairly often. Considering Nick's opinion of his ex-wife, Jenny found it unselfish and admirable that he encouraged his daughter to continue her warm relationship with Marcia's mother.

Nick's contribution was a 35 mm. camera. He instructed Kitty to practice using it so that she would be able to take good pictures at the Grand Canyon. The promised airplane ride was the rest of her tenth birthday present.

For all the attention that was lavished on the child, Jenny found her remarkably unspoiled. But then, her life with her mother seemed to have been far from ideal. There were all those boyfriends, for one thing, and sporadic battles between Nick and Marcia. Jenny told herself that Marcia had been a fool. She had been lucky enough to be Nick's wife, yet she had obviously hurt him deeply. How could she have wanted anyone but her husband?

"You're very quiet tonight, my dear." This from Dr. Hermann, as they sat in the living room after Kitty had opened her presents. Jenny looked up in embarrassment. "I was thinking about a bracelet I'm going to make," she lied. "Hopi overlay. I have to sketch the design."

In fact, she had been thinking about Nick. She knew he was capable of loving deeply—his relationship with his family proved it. So why couldn't he see how much he would gain by giving that love and loyalty to a wife who loved him as she did?

Kitty had been chattering about the Grand Canyon since Labor Day weekend, always assuming that Jenny would be coming along. But Nick never mentioned it until the day of Kitty's party for her school friends, which took place on the Saturday following her birthday. The celebration took the form of a splash party in Nick's pool, and the Hermanns and Jenny were present to chaperone the two dozen boisterous guests.

Jenny was lying on a lounge chair watching the children play in the pool when Nick came over and sat by her feet. For a while they talked companionably about Kitty: how she was adjusting to school and life in Scottsdale, whether he should permit her to spend part of the Christmas holidays with her grandmother in Los Angeles. Although Nick was careful to avoid any reference to his first marriage, he had begun to consult Jenny about decisions affecting Kitty. She was human enough to feel flattered, and so in love with him that any expression of trust or caring left her starry-eyed.

His "Coming to the Grand Canyon with us next weekend?" was inserted so smoothly that Jenny almost said "Sure" without even thinking.

She checked the response just in time. "I can't," she said.

"Why not? Kitty wants you along." His smile was wicked. "I won't seduce you Jenny. I promise to control myself."

"But you'd like to," Jenny blurted out.

"I don't think I need to keep repeating how much I want you. You know how I feel." The smile broadened into a grin. "You know, Jenny, once there was a company I wanted. The price I offered was more than generous, but the owners wouldn't sell out. I had to wait three years until I could engineer a takeover, but now I own that company. I can be patient when I have to be."

The meaning was all too clear. "Well you don't own *me*, now or ever," Jenny said vehemently.

"I don't want to *own* you sweetheart," Nick laughed. "For the moment, it's enough if you come to the Canyon. It means a lot to Kitty."

It was the most unscrupulous sort of blackmail, in Jenny's opinion, to use the child's wishes as a club over her head. She had no doubt that Kitty wanted her to come. But she knew that Nick's primary concern wasn't to please his daughter.

They left for Sedona the following Friday afternoon. In the end, Jenny had agreed to go, but not for Kitty and certainly not to please Nick. She went because she was in love with Nick and wanted to be with him.

The scenery during the first part of their trip, north on the main highway, was much like the other desert terrain Jenny had crossed. Although the stately saguaro cacti were absent, there was the usual array of dark green brush, hay-colored grasses and other cacti, such as prickly pear.

It was only after they had been traveling several miles along the secondary road leading to Sedona that the magnificent scenery which had so enchanted Oscar Hermann became visible. The weather in this mountain country was stormy; soon it began to drizzle. The road meandered between cliffs composed of craggy, striated rock in shades ranging from brown to pink to a striking deep red. Pine, juniper and aspen trees clung to the sides of these rock formations, their green foliage contrasting vividly with the red shades of the rock. As they drove, the rain turned from a few sporadic drops to a full-fledged thunderstorm. Streaks of lightning lit up the sky, zigzagging down to the tops of tall, spectacular peaks.

In the area around Sedona, houses dotted the lower expanses of the red hills. Jenny was amused when Nick cut off the main road to a back lane leading to one of these homes. The man seemed to have a penchant for living on the sides of mountains.

The house was built of redwood and glass, the materials blending beautifully with the natural colors of the rocks and evergreens. Like his house in Scottsdale, the home was built on two levels, but here the pitch of the hill was sharper, so that the floors of the bedrooms upstairs were almost level with the ceilings of the living room and kitchen downstairs.

Over the next day and a half, Jenny was aware of a change in Nick's attitude. He dropped the impersonal charm and sophistication in favor of a warmth and openness he had never before displayed, and seemed endearingly eager for Jenny and Kitty to enjoy themselves.

After dinner at a local restaurant on Friday night, they came back to the house where Nick made a fire in the brick fireplace. He sipped brandy while Jenny and Kitty drank hot chocolate, and the three of them sat and talked until the child fell asleep with her head on her father's lap. Jenny and Nick continued the conversation until long past midnight, speaking of such serious matters as their goals in life and the different ways people searched for fulfillment and happiness. The discussion was intensely personal yet strangely abstract.

They left at nine the next morning, stopping en route for breakfast. Past Sedona, the road was cut through deep canyons and clung to the side of the mountain in a rather alarming manner. They rejoined the highway near Flagstaff, driving the last sixty miles or so through rolling, high pasture where cows and horses grazed contentedly.

Their plane reservations were for a late afternoon flight, so they drove directly to the park. After a stop at the Visitors' Center to look at exhibits on the Canyon's formation, they took a short hike to the rim for their first close view of the multi-hued layers of rock which comprised one of nature's grandest works. Jenny's shortness of breath reminded her that they were 7,000 feet above sea level, the Colorado River still cutting a path through solid rock nearly a mile below.

Then they drove along the south rim, stopping at all the lookouts so Kitty could take pictures. The weather was pleasantly cool, the temperature in the 60's. Jenny stared at the horizontal bands of rock, finding it hard to comprehend that the bottom layer of the gorge was two billion years old. Although the oranges, pinks, browns and reds of the Canyon formations were stunning, she found herself thinking that the Red Rock Country near Sedona was more beautiful. Perhaps the sheer size of the Canyon—up to 18 miles in width and 227 river miles long—lessened its visual impact.

After a late lunch they drove to the airport for the aerial tour Kitty so looked forward to. The Grand Canyon Airlines Cessna held ten people, including the pilot, and everyone had a window seat. Kitty used up an entire roll of film during the fifty minute flight. The pilot pointed out rock formations and waterfalls, the most spectacular of these being Bridal Veil Falls near an Indian village on the Canyon floor. The water was a cool, startling green which contrasted sharply with the brown of the Colorado River. The oasis below was so refreshingly pastoral that Jenny found it hard to believe that summer temperatures in the Inner Canyon desert soared to well above 100°. On their way back Jenny noticed lightning flashing down from a distant thundercloud, a scene Kitty tried to capture on film.

Nick suggested that they postpone dinner until they arrived in Sedona, and both Jenny and Kitty slept most of the way back, waking up as Nick pulled up to a restaurant. It had been a delightful day and Jenny looked forward to reexperiencing the warmth and closeness of the previous evening. She was acutely disappointed when, after dinner, Nick announced that he had several reports to skim and planned to go to bed afterward.

He made a fire for Jenny and Kitty, who stayed downstairs to chat and read until eleven. By then Kitty was yawning continually and Jenny decided that she might as well go to bed also. As they passed Nick's door, she noticed no strip of light underneath. He had gone to sleep.

Chapter Ten

Jenny lay on her back, staring at the ceiling. After a restless hour in bed she had finally dozed off, only to be awakened by a loud snort from Kitty. Resigned to insomnia, she pulled a matching robe on over her sheer nightgown and went downstairs in search of a cold drink.

She found a small can of tomato juice in the refrigerator, and sat down at the dinette table to drink it. It was no use—her afternoon nap made sleep impossible. Several booklets and brochures about the Grand Canyon sat on the living room coffee table, and Jenny decided to go in and glance through them.

When she clicked on the lamp next to the couch, she almost jumped out of her skin. Nick was sitting in one of the armchairs, staring at her. "I'm glad you got up," he said softly. "I was thinking of coming upstairs to wake you."

"Is something wrong?" Jenny sat down on the couch and curled her legs underneath her.

"No. I want to talk to you, that's all. About my first marriage."

Jenny could not imagine why he had decided to speak of something he had once told her was none of her business. But she was aching to hear about it. She made no reply, but simply waited for Nick to continue.

"I was eighteen when my father died," he began, his voice a monotone. "In another month I was due to start college—Dartmouth. But I couldn't leave my mother to run the business by herself, so I stayed in Scottsdale and went to school at Arizona State, where Oscar teaches. I worked a forty hour week and went to school almost full-time, which didn't leave time for anything else. Believe it or not, at your age I was almost as innocent as you are. Not about business—I learned to be tough after a few alleged friends stabbed us in the back—but about women. I was twenty-two when I met Marcia. She was thirty years old, a former model and, although I didn't know it at the time, the shop she owned was a parting gift from a wealthy lover. I'd gone there to buy a birthday present for my mother, and Marcia must have thought it was Christmas and her birthday combined when I walked in. I ended up with a $200 outfit, and wildly infatuated with her. She was beautiful and sophisticated and I'd never met anyone like her. I was scared to death to ask her out and overwhelmed when she accepted."

Nick got up and walked over to a cabinet, withdrawing a bottle of scotch and pouring it into a glass, neat. "After we'd been seeing each other for a few months she told me she was pregnant. Naturally I offered to marry her. My mother did everything she could to stop me, which alienated Marcia and made me more adamant. Kitty was born seven months later."

Jenny thought acidly that the woman hadn't wasted any time in trapping a rich young husband, and Nick's next words confirmed her analysis. "After Kitty's birth I began hearing snide comments—that it was lucky she looked so much like me, at least I could be sure she was mine. I found out that Marcia had been sleeping with two other men at the time she became pregnant with Kitty. One was married, the other was a teacher. She wanted a wealthy husband, and neither one filled the bill. I think she realized that if she didn't nail me, I'd eventually lose interest."

Nick had been pacing slowly back and forth, sipping his drink. He topped off the glass and sat down again. "Two years after we were married, I found out why she wanted me so much. I'd been giving her a huge allowance. I used to wonder what she did with the money, but I never complained because I didn't want any trouble. I felt guilty about spending so much time at school, at work and traveling. But it had to stop—I couldn't afford it. Finally I had the books from her store audited and found she'd been losing money steadily. I gave her a choice: either sell out, or sell a controlling interest to AMT and accept a professional manager/buyer. The things she carried were more suited to Beverly Hills than Phoenix. She made the changes but she hated me for it. Until then we had managed to coexist, but at that point she started seeing other men. The marriage was over, but I didn't want to lose Kitty, so I put up with it. When Kitty was four, Marcia left me. She went to Los Angeles to be closer to her mother.

"At that point I filed for divorce. I began to acquire

more business interests in California, and eventually we opened an office in L.A. I went there a few times a month on business, and took Kitty for weekends. All in all, Marcia and I got along fairly smoothly. Whatever her faults, she was a good mother and she loved Kitty. She always had a lot of men, but she never let them stay over. Then she met Paul. When I found out he was living with her, I raised the roof. I threatened to sue for custody. Marcia told me they were going to marry, but I'd wised up in ten years and had the guy investigated. He was an out-of-work actor with a rich wife and three kids. He'd lived with girlfriends before, and he always went back to his wife. When I confronted Marcia with that, she was furious. We had a violent argument, with me screaming that I was taking Kitty back to Scottsdale and Marcia screaming that Kitty wasn't even my daughter. Kitty was upstairs, and she heard the whole thing.''

Now Jenny understood the child's doubts about her parentage. ''Kitty ran downstairs, crying,'' Nick continued, still nursing the scotch. ''At that point, I grabbed her and left. I took her out for the day; a freak summer storm blew in so we went to a movie and then back to Marcia's. By the time we got there, she was dead.''

Jenny was stunned. The story sounded like a soap opera script. ''What happened?'' she whispered.

''Marcia was upset, probably over what I'd told her about Paul. She wasn't much of a sailor, but she took his small boat out. When the storm hit, she got into trouble. A neighbor saw her and called the Coast Guard, but by the time they got there all they found was wreckage. Her body washed up the next day.''

He gulped the rest of the scotch and sat silently, apparently lost in thought. After several minutes Jenny asked softly, "Why are you telling me this now, when you wouldn't before?"

"I want you, Jenny." His smile was brittle. "I had the patience to wait three years for that company I told you about, but a molybdenum mine doesn't prance around the kitchen in a bikini. My self-control is about shot. Since you don't seem to like the idea of sleeping with me unless we're married, I want you to marry me. I figured you had to know about Marcia if you were ever going to understand me."

Nick left his seat to join Jenny on the couch, pulling her close and kissing her gently on the mouth. She felt his pain acutely; he was no longer the arrogant, self-confident man she had met seven weeks ago, but twenty-two years old, naive and vulnerable. She wanted to comfort him. She put her arms around him and hugged him, rubbing his back soothingly.

Jenny's robe had no buttons or zipper, just a sash which Nick untied. He slipped her nightgown from her shoulders, leaving her bare to the waist, and bent his head to begin a slow, sensual teasing of her breasts which left her feverish with pleasure. Then his mouth was on hers, kissing her, at first tenderly and then with a smoldering passion. Jenny's emotions veered between maternal tenderness and melting submissiveness. Nick took his mouth away and pushed her down on the couch to lie beside him, and Jenny buried her head in his neck. "Oh Nick," she murmured, "I love you so much."

"I know," Nick whispered, stroking her hair. "I once told you I cared for you and would make you happy, Jen. And I will; I don't want to make the same mistake twice. I'll never dictate to you, I promise. The jewelry you make is beautiful, and I expect you'll want to continue working. But whatever you decide is fine with me."

But Jenny wanted more from a man than caring and financial support. "I said I love you, Nick," she repeated.

There was no reply. Jenny felt a numbing apprehension. "And you?" she asked softly.

He gently kissed her mouth, then drew slightly away to study her face. His expression was very solemn. "I told you how I feel. It's the best I can do."

Apprehension turned to stabbing pain. Jenny's eyes moistened as she silently shook her head.

"You're too young and too romantic," Nick insisted. "It will work, believe me. Part of the reason I wanted you to come along this weekend was to see what it would be like if you and I and Kitty were a family. It was terrific, Jenny."

Jenny was filled with a poignant sadness for what she might have had but never would. She loved Nick desperately, but could never marry him, knowing what she did. Tears rolling down her face, she told him why. "I may be young and romantic, but I'm smarter than you are, Nick. My parents' friends—the ones with the perfect marriages—I've seen them fall apart, right and left. Even when two people love each other, it seems hard to stay together. And you don't love me. You'd end up hating me for insisting on marriage. It would be a disaster, just like your marriage to Marcia. I can't cope with that kind of pain. And I can't do that to you."

Nick sat up; Jenny did likewise. "I don't believe you mean that, Jenny. You can't mean that if you love me."

She shook her head sadly. "You're wrong. It's just because I *do* love you that I can't let it happen." With trembling fingers she slipped her gown and robe back on and left the room.

Jenny cried for most of the night. She wanted to believe that Nick would come to love her if they married, but she was afraid to take the chance. His scars were so deep; she wasn't confident enough to feel she could heal them. She knew that if she stayed in Scottsdale, she would become either his mistress or his wife, only to go through hell when his infatuation with her waned.

There was no choice but to leave. Nick was bitingly impatient the next morning, regarding her drawn face and puffy eyes with angry disgust. Kitty, who had begun the morning achatter with enthusiasm about the trip, soon lapsed into a depressed silence.

Nick dropped Jenny off at the Hermanns', but didn't come inside. Marian took one look at Jenny's ravaged face and called Oscar, then fixed coffee for all of them. As they sat in the living room, Jenny haltingly spoke of her decision to leave, offering to stay on until they found a replacement. When pressed for an explanation, she told them the truth.

Oscar shook his head impatiently. "Jenny, my dear, Nicholas is obviously . . ." he began, then thought better of it. If she wanted to leave, he said, he and Marian would make it as easy as possible for her. They would invite Nick to dinner Monday night and tell him of her decision; she could go to a movie or work in the shop to avoid being present. Marian volunteered to take care of Kitty until Jenny left.

For the next two days Jenny threw herself into her work, finishing both a necklace and a bracelet. She told the Barbers she was leaving and arranged to continue to send them her jewelry from Davis. By the time she got back to the Hermanns' Monday evening, it was nearly midnight and everyone was asleep.

Tuesday was easily the worst day of her life. She had no more work to preoccupy her. No one seemed to care that she was leaving. Marian Hermann told her over dinner that she had already found a replacement; Jenny could go as soon as she had packed up. Kitty, who was eating with them, looked as chipper as ever. "Gee Jenny," she said, "I'm really going to miss you." But she didn't sound it.

Worst of all, Nick was totally impersonal. Jenny couldn't bear the thought of leaving without saying good-bye to him, so when he came to pick up Kitty late Tuesday evening, she walked the child out to the car. She managed a hoarse good-bye, knowing that she was really hoping that Nick would say or do something to make her change her mind. But he only smiled distantly and told her to give his regards to her father.

She left early the next morning. Marian Hermann had insisted on making reservations at AMT's motor inn in Indio, and Jenny was too stricken to protest that the memories of that place would be too painful. She was so numb with grief that it didn't seem to matter. Nothing seemed to matter.

She arrived midafternoon, forced herself to eat a late lunch, and spent the rest of the day at the pool talking to strangers and trying to forget that she felt so lonely and miserable that she wanted to cut out the part of her brain that controlled her emotions. She wanted to be a zombie, apparently alive but feeling nothing.

In the evening, she tried to watch television but couldn't concentrate on the simplest comedy plot.

Finally she decided to take a long, hot bath, hoping it would help her relax enough to get some sleep. She was emotionally exhausted; she couldn't possibly drive to Bakersfield if she didn't get some rest.

Perhaps it was the thought of an earlier incident in an Indio motel room that made Jenny decide to lock the door from the inside. Or perhaps it was a strange sensation of being watched. She was distressed to find the chain broken, but forced herself to ignore her fear and take her bath. She didn't need paranoia in addition to all her other problems.

When she emerged almost an hour later, a towel wrapped around her body, she knew something was wrong. She had left the bedside lamp on, and now the room was dark. Her heart began to pound in alarm and for several moments she stood rooted to the carpet in terror. Somebody was in the room, she was sure of it. The phone was next to the bed, so her only hope of escape was to bolt out the door. Then the light clicked back on again and Jenny almost fainted with shock.

"Jenny? Come to bed, honey." It was Nick's voice and Jenny wanted to kill him for frightening her so badly. Oblivious to the fact that she wore only a towel, she stormed around the wall which hid the bed from view. He was lying there, the blankets pulled up only to his waist, revealing a bare chest. And he had the most maddening smirk on his face.

"What do you think you're doing?" she raged. "You scared the wits out of me. What are you, some kind of sadist? Or are you just crazy?"

"Probably the latter," Nick laughed. "Men in love often are. Now come to bed, darling."

All the anger drained out of Jenny, to be replaced by the worst anxiety she had ever experienced. Men in love? Did he mean that? Or was he just telling her that because he was intent on marrying her and getting her to bed.

"I said I love you, Jenny," Nick repeated. "Come to bed and we'll talk. I'd prefer it if you'd exchange the towel for nothing," he added wickedly, "but put on a nightgown if you feel you have to."

In a daze, Jenny took a nightgown and robe from her overnight case, went into the bathroom to slip them on, and returned to stand by the bed. She couldn't bring herself to slip between the sheets. "What are you doing here?" she whispered.

"I just told you I love you. Isn't it obvious why I'm here? Come to bed, Jennifer, because if you don't, I'm going to come after you, and I'm not wearing a thing."

When Jenny hesitated, Nick began to lift the covers. She hastily scrambled into the queen-size bed, saying warily, "You promise not to touch me?"

"For the time being," Nick agreed. "I suppose I should apologize for scaring you, but it's your own fault. If you had been at dinner on Monday, I would have proposed again and I could have told you what you needed to hear. When you refused to marry me, I didn't believe it at first. Then I was angry." Nick's voice softened and gentled. "By Monday morning I knew I wanted you to share my life. I've never loved anyone except my family, Jenny, and it took me a while to realize that what I feel for you is as intense as what I feel for them—more intense, in some ways." He paused, his expression thoughtful. "After Marcia left, I think I chose women I could never love, just to avoid emotional entanglements. I told every one of them I wasn't interested in marriage, and they always appeared to accept it. Maybe some of them figured they could change my mind, but no one ever did. Until you."

Jenny sat propped up by a pillow with her arms huddled in front of her. She wanted to believe what she was hearing, but it was so difficult after what she had been through. "But—but Saturday night you said the opposite. You were so definite. How can I be sure?"

"You can't," Nick answered. "You'll have to trust me." Then he reached over and began to play with her hair, twining a strand around his fingers. "I've told you things I've never told anyone, Jenny. I feel very close to you. In the beginning it was a game, and then pure desire, but there was a point where you stopped blowing up every five minutes and I think that's when I stopped seeing you as a provocative little source of amusement and began to fall in love with you."

His tender look was all the additional reassurance Jenny needed. She lifted her hand to cover his, only to have it seized, a gentle kiss pressed into its palm.

"I've had the most awful four days. How could you do that to me?" she pouted.

"I couldn't resist, darling. Monday night I told everyone how we'd met—an edited version, because Kitty was there. And when I was telling them about it, I knew that I had to propose again in Indio. I suppose my family shares my warped sense of humor, because nobody tried to talk me out of it. Why do you think Mom insisted on this motel? And why do you think you've got a room with a queen-size bed?"

Jenny blushed furiously. "Your mother—"

"Is very human, just like us," Nick finished.

"How did you know when to come into the room? I felt like someone was watching me—"

"Through the curtains. I thought you'd never go into

the bathroom. You noticed, of course, that I made sure the chain lock was broken."

"You're impossible," Jenny giggled.

"But you love me."

"Yes, I love you," she agreed.

"And you're going to marry me tomorrow," Nick said firmly. "It's all arranged."

"I thought you weren't going to try to run my life, Nicholas," Jenny protested, not minding in the least.

"We're driving to Vegas in the morning. My family and your family will meet us."

Jenny couldn't resist a gentle gibe. "My father must be pleased. And you—you've found yourself the perfect father-in-law."

She was surprised when Nick took the dart seriously. She knew her father's position had nothing to do with Nick's feelings for her. "Damn it," he said with annoyance, "if I wanted to marry a woman with a powerful father, I could have married Joanna."

"Speaking of Joanna . . ." Jenny put in.

"I wasn't very nice that night, was I?" Nick admitted. "I was half in love with you and I suppose it terrified me. I like to be in control, but whenever you were at the house I had trouble keeping my distance. I tried coolness and you ignored it. Taking you out to lunch was a disaster, I had trouble even concentrating on the conversation. As for flaunting Joanna . . . I meant to put you off by implying that we were still lovers, but from the time I met you I never touched her. She left five minutes after you did."

"You were horrible to me for the next week," Jenny reminded him, delighted by his admission.

"I knew you were in love with me, but I didn't know what to do about it. All my instincts told me to run, but

every time I hurt you I felt like such a louse. I was
jealous of Jim Maloma—"

"I never went out with him," Jenny interrupted. "I
made it up to avoid you."

"Did you?" Nick seemed amused.

Jenny nodded and smiled.

"Well you didn't make up all the men who were
leering at you the night of the party. By the time I came
into the cabana I felt like having you no matter what.
Except," he teased, "I knew I could have your full
cooperation."

"So why didn't you just seduce me?" Jenny questioned. "Was it because of my father?"

"No. Once I'd made up my mind to have you, I told
myself it was only a matter of time until you agreed,
because you loved me. It was easier to be patient. Over
the next few weeks I began to feel that marriage wasn't
such a bad idea, and you know the rest. Kitty is
ecstatic, by the way. She's crazy about you, just like her
father."

Jenny sighed with contentment at his declaration of
love. "Just think, Nick. If Oscar's cousin hadn't known
about the job, I never would have—"

"Not true," Nick said with a tender smile. "I would
have met you eventually even if you hadn't come to
Scottsdale. After that party, your father asked me to
come to dinner next time I was in Sacramento on
business. He wanted to introduce us. After he de-
scribed you I realized you were the one I'd been staring
at at your grandmother's party. I certainly had no
objections."

"So it was fated," Jenny joked. "I find that terribly
romantic."

Nick responded by moving closer, until his body half

covered Jenny's. To her relief, she felt denim rather than bare skin against her legs.

"You're wearing—"

The sentence was cut off by the feather-light kisses Nick was planting on her mouth. "And do you find this terrible romantic also, darling?" he whispered against her lips.

Jenny reacted to his lovemaking with passionate longing, and was about to twine her arms around his neck and return his kisses when a picture flashed into her mind: her own parents and the Hermanns having dinner together in Las Vegas, discussing the impending wedding.

"You can't stay here," she protested guiltily, trying to wiggle away. "You'll have to stay in another room."

Nick rolled off her and sat up. "Are you serious?" he demanded irritably. "You really want to stop *now?*"

"Please, Nick. It's only another day. I can't spend the night with you and then face my parents and your—"

"Is that the only reason?"

He sounded so annoyed that Jenny began to tremble. Of course she wanted Nick to make love to her, but she preferred to be his wife first. She was trying to find the right words to express her feelings when he muttered, "I should have taken my jeans off!" Then he added in a louder tone, "Okay, if it makes you happy, get your pretty backside into the bathroom and put some clothes on. We're leaving."

"Leaving?" Jenny repeated in confusion. "Just because I won't—"

"There's no way I can calmly walk out of this room and fall asleep next door, Jenny." Nick got out of bed and grabbed his shirt, quickly buttoning it and tucking it into his jeans. "Come on, Jen! Don't just lie there, unless it's an invitation. I'm not made of stone."

His words had the intended effect. Jenny scrambled out of bed, pulled some clothing from her suitcase and fled into the bathroom to change. She couldn't imagine where he planned to go at this time of night.

Her speculations were interrupted by two loud raps on the door; Nick immediately opened it up and strolled in. The next moment, Jenny found herself in his arms, her mouth captured in a rough, burning kiss that ended as abruptly as it had started.

"That will have to hold me until we get to Vegas." To Jenny's amusement, Nick sounded extremely disgruntled about it.

She slept while he drove, waking up just as they reached Las Vegas to be informed by Nick that he had no intention of waiting until that afternoon to make her his wife.

"Get married *now*?" Jenny questioned sleepily. "But it's the middle of the night."

"There's no such thing as the middle of the night in Vegas," Nick retorted. "It's a twenty-four-hour town."

By dawn, Nick had slipped a gold band onto Jenny's finger, coaxed her into eating breakfast, and won $50 after nonchalantly flipping a few half-dollars into a handy slot machine. They checked into AMT's hotel, receiving a raft of congratulations and one or two sly grins when Nick announced that they had just been married. After escorting Jenny to the luxurious bridal suite, he immediately informed her that he had an important errand to run.

Feeling somewhat abandoned, she decided to shower away the clamminess resulting from having slept in her clothes most of the night. She was rinsing shampoo from her hair when she heard the sound of the heavy shower door rolling open. Rubbing the water from her eyes, she opened them to see a full champagne glass next to her nose.

Now that Jenny understood where Nick had gone, she didn't mind at all. "In the shower?" she giggled.

"Why not?" Nick stripped off his clothing and stepped inside, his hand clutching his own glass of champagne, his eyes registering amusement at Jenny's fascinated but embarrassed inspection.

"To us," he murmured, clicking his glass against Jenny's. She obediently sipped the bubbling liquid, hardly tasting it. Looking at Nick made her dizzy with excitement. She was his wife and she couldn't wait for him to take her in his arms and begin making love to her.

She was given no choice. A moment later he removed her glass from her hand and set it, along with his own, on the sink. Although she was already clean, he insisted on lathering every inch of her body, his hands stroking and caressing until Jenny clutched at him in frustration. Finally she was permitted a single, tantalizing kiss.

She only realized that Nick was toying with her when he pulled his mouth away and reached for his razor. He was maddeningly deliberate about shaving, and in no apparent hurry to make love to her afterward, either. He pulled her back against the hardness of his body, his hands cupping her breasts, his mouth nuzzling her neck.

Several minutes of this teasing was all Jenny could endure. She leaned weakly backward, moaning achingly, *"Please,* Nick."

In reply, he switched off the shower, stepped out and

tossed Jenny a towel. As both of them dried themselves, he yawned and stretched. "Gee, I'm tired," he said. "After a 300 mile drive, I need some sleep."

"Are you serious?" Jenny asked incredulously, her body longing for fulfillment. "You want to stop *now?*"

Nick's mouth quirked into a smile, then quickly straightened. "Now where," he asked drily, "have I heard that before?"

Jenny stared at the floor, scarlet at the realization that he had used exactly those words only a few hours ago in Indio. Now she knew what it must have cost Nick to accede to her wishes, and loved him all the more for his consideration. Perhaps he really was exhausted, she thought guiltily.

"I understand," she murmured dejectedly, stepping out of the shower. "I guess I can wait." She knew she would be unable to sleep. She would probably spend the next few hours staring at Nick, longing for him to wake up.

"Well I can't!" There was laughter mixed with the words, causing Jenny to jerk her head up and study the expression in her husband's eyes. She saw both love and impatience, and with an enticing smile reached out her arms to Nick, who picked her up and carried her to bed.

Silhouette Romance

ROMANCE THE WAY
IT USED TO BE...
AND COULD BE AGAIN

Contemporary romances for today's women

*Each month, six very special love stories will
be yours from SILHOUETTE. Look for them
wherever books are sold or order now
from the coupon below.*

$1.50 each

Silhouette Romance

SILHOUETTE BOOKS, Department SB/1

1230 Avenue of the Americas, New York, N.Y. 10020

Please send me the books I have checked above. I am enclosing $_____
(please add 50¢ to cover postage and handling for each order. N.Y.S. and N.Y.C.
residents please add appropriate sales tax). Send check or money order—no
cash or C.O.D.s please. Allow up to six weeks for delivery.

NAME_____

ADDRESS_____

CITY_____ STATE/ZIP_____

READERS' COMMENTS ON SILHOUETTE ROMANCES:

"Every one was written with the utmost care. The story of each captures one's interest early in the plot and holds it all through until the end."

—P.B.,* Summersville, West Virginia

"Silhouette Books are so refreshing that they take you into different worlds. . . . They bring love, happiness and romance into my life. I hope Silhouette goes on forever."

—B.K., Mauldin, South Carolina

"What I really enjoy about your books is they happen in different parts of the U.S.A. and various parts of the world. . . ."—P.M., Tulia, Texas

"I was happy to see another romance-type book available on the market—Silhouette—and look forward to reading them all."

—E.N., Washington, D.C.

"The Silhouette Romances are done exceptionally well. They are so descriptive . . ."

—F.A., Golden, Colorado

* names available on request